Korean Traditional Desserts

Ricecakes, Cookies and Beverages

By **Sook-Ja YOON**
Professor of Baewha Women's College

Translation by **Young-Hie HAN**
Proofreading by Glasgow **L. REYNOLDS**
Professors of Dankook University

JI-GU Publishing Co.
Seoul, Korea

Korean Traditional Desserts : Ricecakes, Cookies and Beverages

written by Sook-Ja Yoon
Professor of Baewha Women' College
Translation by Young-Hie Han
Proofreading by Glasgow L. Reynolds
Proffessor of Dankook University
Published by Byung-Oh Joo

'ublished by Ji-Gu Publishing©1979
518-2 Paju Bookcity
Munbal-li Ghoha-up Paju-si
Gyonggi-do, KOREA

This edition first published 1998
second impression 2000
English, Japan edition 2001

ISBN 89-7006-239-4

All rights reserved. No part of this publication may be reproduced, stoved in a retrieval system, or transmitted in any way or by any means, electronic, mechanical, photocopying, recording or otherwise, without the prior written permission of the copyright holder.

ISBN 89-7006-239-4

Foreword and Acknowledgements

I am pleasn mores and customs is Korean food. With the shrinking world into thed to present this English book on Korean ricecake, pastry and beverages to those who reside in the English speaking regions, in response to their demand of and their interests in Korean cuisine; simultaneously with the Japanese version to the Japanese.

One of the most representative Koreae so-called global village, various indigenous and characteristic foods are now available and many people are interested in them across the national borders. Korean cooking is one of them and has been emerging from obscurity to the fore.

At present there are only very few Korean cookbooks in English available in the market. So it is worthwhile to add this edition for those interested in Korean cuisine.

The most characteristic aspect of the Korean food lies in the fact that the natural taste and flavor of the materials used in cooking are preserved maximally, and dishes are prepared very elaborately. We find that even the Korean traditional *ttŏk* with a history of several thousand years, is a mirror of Korean customs and believe that it is very unique from Western bread and cakes in many respects.

In terms of the materials in *ttŏk* alone, it is very proportionate in its tastes, nutrition, and flavor and shows a very reasonable combination of materials. This can also be found in many kinds of desserts and drinks.

For example, starch food rice is combined with various protein and fat food items, such as bean, chestnut, jujube, walnut and pinenut. Added to these natural and wholesome foods are dried fruits, mugwort, angelica, stone mushroom, *bokryung* pine root mushroom (Wolfiporia cocos), *ch'angch'ul* root(Atractylis chinensis), seaside pinenut, and taro. Proper combinations of most of them are scientifically proved to provide invigorating functions to the body.

Other additions of nutrients are from azalea, chrysanthemum, rose, cinnamon, pine pollen, black sesame, pine endodermis, five-flavor seed, gardenia seed, rouge, and *chich'u*, turmeric. Most of these are also used as coloring agents in pastry, mutually complementary and excellent nutrients necessary to bodily functions.

To reiterate, they are not only natural and herbal foods excellent to the physiological function of the body, but also enticing visually and palatably. Furthermore their elaborate utilization seems to put the Korean eating customs and culture a step higher from their daily necessities.

On the other hand, there are various local distinctions in foods; each local food represents its produce, needs, the liking and emotion of the local people through the form, size, taste, color, flavor, and materials; for example, in North Korea, they prepare fermented and fried cereal cake *not'i* for longer preservation and body energy source in the cold winter.

To make ricecake more enticing to the eyes, people put some decorations on it, by which the ricecake looks more palatable. The beauty of *juak* and *whajŏn* which are used as decorations to *pyun* is very exquisite, representing the beautiful harmony of human and nature as a single unit. This seems to represent our philosophy of life and gives satisfaction to onlookers and eaters alike.

However, we have witnessed these days the trend that our eating habit is being much Westernized or fusion food is coming to the scene among our young folks in line with the huge influx of the Western cultures, neglecting our own traditions; as such, our traditional ricecakes and desserts are disappearing from our daily life. We view that it is our duty to realize and enhance the true value of Korean traditional indigenous foods, which have taken quite a long time to take the present forms, and we should learn, keep, refine and elaborate it and further inherit it to our posterity and provide it to the world.

We believe that such an act is to be the basics for our cultural development and creativeness within the world heritage. In our modern society where our living is heading only for something speedy, convenient, and economical, the effort to keep our traditional food of ricecake and pastry in our modern living is a meritorious act for preserving our unique traditional culture.

This book is originally written based on the exploration into earlier written documents and common practices among the folks, my lectures in college, cooking experiences and the enthusiastic help of my students. They are arranged to give handy recipes with which Korean pastries can be made conveniently. However, there may be many shortcomings in this book, to which I solicit your candid advice and criticism to make the next version more lucid and concise.

There are many individuals and institutions that have contributed to the publication of the original book and its English version. But my special thanks are extended to, first of all, my husband, President Jeong-Hwan CHOI of the IMFITRON for financial assistance and incessant suggestions and my son Min-Gu for his encouragements from Hawaii; Prof. Young-Hie HAN and Prof. Glasgow L. REYNOLDS of Dankook University, for translating and proofreading; and Mr. Kyung-Taek LEE of the Hanwool Photo Research Lab for taking excellent and illustrative pictures on cooking; Reporter Mr. Duck-Hun PARK of the monthly magazine, *Shikseangwhal*(Eating Life) for helping me write series on food; President Byung-Oh JOO and editors of the Jigu Publishing Co., for taking up the publication of this book with some uncertainty of circulation; and finally the staffmembers of my Korean Traditional Food Research Circle and many others who have contributed behind the scene to make this book possible. Without their help and contribution, this book would still be in the planning stage.

March 2001

Sook-Ja Yun

Translator's Note

In order to give readability to the English readers, an English equivalent is given first before its Korean indigenous word is presented. That is, terms of Korean food are given in English as far as possible. The equivalent Korean terms are given after the English ones or in the parentheses, believing that Korean terms are not familiar to most non-Koreans.

In translating Korean terms, the translator referred to Prof. Woul Young Chu's *From Traditional Korean Cuisine*, published in 1985 by The Korea Times, L. A. and Kyo Hak Sa, Seoul; and Profs. E Soon Choi and Ki Yull Lee's *Practical Korean Recipes*, published in 1976 by The Yonsei University Press, Seoul. Choi and Lee report that an earlier English Korean cookbook, *Korean Recipes*, was written by Harriett Morris and published in 1940 after she had returned to her hometown, Wichita, Kansas, after teaching at Ewha Woman's University. The author and the translator of this English version are thankful to the authors of the above two books.

However, in some cases, the translator chose or concocted English equivalent terms that he thinks proper and adequate; about which further consideration will be given as far as possible.

It is often difficult for the translator to give an exact English term equivalent to its original Korean term, which stems from two reasons: one reason is that he can't find adequate terms in other Korean cookery books in English, where Korean terms are usually given in Roman alphabet followed by an explanation of its meaning, or even if they are given in English equivalents, they are all different from each other, from one cookery book to another; the other reason is that he is not fully familiar with English confectionary and bakery terms so that he may not have been able to utilize the possible closest equivalents.

Romanization of the Korean Alphabet

In this book, the McCune-Reischauer's Romanization system is used, although it has diacritics, such as ŏ and ŭ to represent central mid and unrounded back high vowels, respectively(Cf. Various Korean Romanization systems listed in page X of Samuel E. Martin, Yang Ha Lee, and Sung Ung Chang's New *Korean English Dictionary*(韓美大辭典), published in 1976 by Minjungseogwan, Seoul, and the Yale University Press, New Haven, Conn.).

The equivalents of the Korean Hangul to the Roman alphabet according to McCuine and Reischauer are as follows:

ㅂ : p, b	ㄱ : k, g	ㅣ : i	ㅓ : ŏ
ㅍ : p'	ㅋ : k'	ㅟ : wi	ㅕ : yŏ
ㅃ : pp	ㄲ : kk	ㅔ : e	ㅝ : wŏ
ㄷ : t, d	ㅁ : m	ㅖ : yc	ㅏ : a
ㅌ : t'	ㄴ : n	ㅞ : we	ㅑ : ya
ㄸ : tt	ㅇ : -ng	ㅚ : oe	ㅘ : wa
ㅅ : s	ㄹ : l, r	ㅐ : ae	ㅜ : u
ㅆ : ss	ㅎ : h	ㅒ : yae	ㅠ : yu
ㅈ : ch, j		ㅙ : wae	ㅗ : o
ㅊ : ch'		ㅡ : ŭ	ㅛ : yo
ㅉ : tch		ㅢ : ŭi	

Here the term ricecake is used as a cover term for cereal cakes, because Korean cakes are usually made from rice, although other cereals such as sorghum, Italian millet, barley, corn, etc., are also used.

The term rice, *ssal*, or regular rice is sticky rice consumed as staple food in the Far Eastern countries, such as Korea, Japan and northern China. Therefore, stickier rice, or glutinous rice used in this text means rice far stickier than the regular rice, which is used in the outer crust of Japanese *mochi* cake stuffed with sweetened bean paste.

The term jujube refers to jujube quite common in Korea.

Contents

1. The Origins and Development of Ricecakes

The origins of Korean traditional cereal cake *ttŏk* are assumed to be traceable to the Bronze Age and their developments, to the later stages of the Three Kingdom period; the steaming utensils made of clay for cereal cakes are found in the shell heaps left by the people of the Bronze Age, and in some of the tombs of the Three Kingdoms. In the dwelling places of the ancient people are found without an exception soft-stones and grinding stones(확돌). At the same time in the tomb murals of the Kokuryŏ Kingdom, such as the #3 tomb of Anak and another tomb of Yaksuri, both in Whanghae-do Province, are depicted with people preparing steamed cakes. From these pieces of evidence, it is quite natural to conclude that the ancient people of these periods must have used the instruments to crush or grind cereals in order to make steamed cakes, using steaming vessels.

Cereal cakes are closely related with, and woven into, Korean ways of life. They are prepared in various forms at various festive occasions not only to celebrate the occasions themselves, but also to cherish the custom of sharing food among relatives and neighbors.

On the new year's day by the lunar calendar, white ricecake and soup is prepared; on the first day of February, *chungwhajŏl-pnal*, another kind of half-moon shaped stuffed ricecake, *nobi songpyŏn*, is prepared; on March 3, *samjit-nal*, another kind of fried brier flower cake, *tugyŏn whajŏn*; on April 8, Buddha's birthday, a cake made with zelkova tree leaves, *nŭthittŏk*; on May the 5th, *tano-nal*, a fancy ricecake called *surich'wi* made with fragrant wild aster; on June the 6th, *yutu-nal*, still another kind of *ttŏk*, rice balls in honeyed water garnished with pinenuts, called *sudan ttŏk*; on August Moon Festival, *chusŏk*, which falls on August the 15th, a special delicacy, *songpyŏn*, a half-moon shaped ricecake stuffed with bean paste, chestnuts, jujubes or the like; on the 9th day of the ninth month September, *chunggujŏl*, when two 9s are overlapped, a flower pancake with chrysanthemum's leaves, *kukwhajŏn*; on October the 10th, *chungyangjŏl*, steamed ricecakes, *siruttŏk* with powdered rice in layers separated by redbeans are also prepared and served. On the occasions of family celebrations, such as the birthdays of grown-ups, especially seniors or aged persons; especially on one's sixtieth birthday; on an infant's one-hundredth (survival) day after birth; on the first birthday; on the wedding day; on the forefather worshipping day(as an offering), cereal cakes, especially made from rice are served or offered.

Cereal cakes are used on these days without exception since in them their sacred prayers for their well-being are presumed to be well represented, everyone praying for or expressing the hope that a long and everlasting peace may come to their family and relatives, so that the celebrated person may live happily for a long time to come, or the spirits of their forefathers may find peace.

Ttŏk can be classified according to its cooking methods: steamed *ttŏk*, and steamed and mashed *ttŏk*, fried *ttŏk*, boiled stickier *ttŏk*, etc.

The steamed *tchinttŏk*(甑餠, 蒸餠) is nicknamed *shiru-ttŏk* as it is usually cooked in an earthenware utensil called *siru*. It is prepared with regular or stickier rice, which is soaked sufficiently in fresh water, and then powdered and put into the *siru* for steaming. The steamed ricecake is further subclassified into two kinds according to the methods of steaming: *solkittŏk* and *khŏttŏk*(layered cake); the former is steamed after watering is done sufficiently to the rice powder in the steamer so that the entire rice powder becomes one single mass during steaming; and the latter is steamed after several layers of rice powder demarcated by *komul* comprised of kneaded soft redbeans, are formed.

The pounded cake, *ch'inttŏk*(搗餠), is made in the following fashion: first of all, water-soaked cereal is powdered, then steamed, and pounded in a mortar or on a flat block board. To this category belong the white ricecake, *whinttŏk*; the fancy ricecake *chulphyŏn*; the half-moon shaped cake stuffed with bean jam, *kaephittŏk*; the glutinous ricecake, *injŏlmi*; dumplings stuffed with honey, *tanja*(團子), etc.

The fried variety, *chijinttŏk*(油煎餠), is made of stickier rice powder, which is first of all steamed and fried in various shapes. Of this kind are pancakes, *chŏnbyŏng*(煎餠); fried flower cakes *whajŏn*; fried honey cake, *cuak*, etc. The flower cake *whajŏn* is made in the following fashion: the glutinous rice powder is kneaded into a flat and round form on which flower petals are put and then fried. Season-wise, Koreans have azalea and pear flower frys in the spring, the rose flower fry in the early summer, and the chrysanthemum and cockscomb flower frys in the autumn.

The blanched *ssalmŭnttŏk* dipped in boiling water, is made in the following way: first, glutunous rice flour is kneaded into certain forms by hand, or cut in the form of *cuak* or *yakkwa* or in the form of a pipe, and then dipped in seething water, and scooped for dredging using various kinds of powders. *Kyŏngdan*, *chapkwapyŏng*, *swaepaekja*, *sanyakpyŏng*, *p'ungsopyŏng* belong to this category.

The ubiquitous food *ttŏk* is the most traditional Korea cereal cake, which has, from ancient times, been made and enjoyed as food of yearly festivals and feasting occasions, and as offerings to the forefathers. These occasional cakes are, after rites, given to the relatives and neighbors as a sign of well-wishing and good-heartedness. It can be said that *ttŏk* has been the most indigenous spirit cherishing and indispensable food to the Koreans on various festivals rooted in the traditional worships and shamanism.

Korean Ricecake

Steamed Ricecake

Pounded Cake

Pan-fried Cake

Boiled Ricecake

1. Steamed red-been Ricecake (*P'atkomul Siruttŏk*)

Tchinunttok

Those *siruttŏk* which have been handed down to the present are the *hupyŏng*(厚餠), the *cŭngpyŏng*(蒸餠), the steamed redbean *siruttŏk*, flat soft pastry *p'atp'yŏn*, soft flat glutinous pastry *p'atch'alpyŏn*, *kŭp'i pat mesiruttŏk*, *kŭp'i pat ch'alsiruttŏk*, etc.

According to the book on food, the *Ŭmsik Pangmun*(飲食方文) written in the 1800s, one of the steamed cakes is made in the following fashion, "Make rice powder; mix it with salted water; using a coarse sieve, sift the coarse flour gently. and with another coarse sieve, *komul* made of cereal with husks peeled off, is sifted and placed in the steaming container. The core of jujubes are removed with a knife; the hard skin of boiled chestnuts are removed; and the meat of the chestnuts is placed into the rice flour so as to make each layer evenly formed."

Redbean steamed *ttŏk* is one of the most traditional cakes for offerings to the household god, and also to the village gods or guardian deities in the harvest month of October, *sangtal*, in order to pray for the family's well-being and villagers' peace, prosperity, freedom from diseases and a bountiful harvest in the coming year, especially on the occasion of *tŭngsinjae* when thicker or higher layers of *ttŏk* are usually prepared and shared among villagers.

The regular rice, *mepssal*, is usually used as the main ingredient, but stickier rice, *ch'apssal*, is also preferred so that the denomination of either *mepssal ttŏk* or *ch'apssal ttŏk* is used as another kind of cover term based on the main substance of the *ttŏk*.

As *komul*, demarcator, or the covering is usually made from redbean or green beans; the former is said to be shunned by evil spirits and therefore used in preparing the sacrifice, *kosa ttŏk*, to dispel ghosts, and green beans, as the offerings to one's forefathers and for other festivities.

Materials and quantity

{	plain rice ... 10 cups(20 cups of rice flour)	
	salt	2 Tbsp
{	redbean	6 cups
	salt	2 Tbsp

❶

❷

❸

❹

Recipe

1. Wash rice, immerse it in water for 12 hours, drain off water, add salt to the soaked rice and pound it into a powder, sift the powder to get finer rice flour (If the powder is lacking in moisture, spray water over the powder, and rub it with both hands, sifting it again.).
2. Boil up the redbean in fresh water, drain off the water, add fresh water three times as much as the redbean and boil it again until it becomes soft, then drain off the water and place the redbean over weak heat again for maturing. Add salt to it and pound it in mortar to make dredging.
3. Place a steam screen pad on the bottom of the *siru* steamer, then spread the redbean dredging over the screen and put rice powder over it, 3 or 4 cm thick. Then the redbean dredging and rice powder layers are placed alternately, until the redbean layer comes to the top. Place the steamer over a kettle, placing steam blocker paste made of the rice powder to prevent steam from leaking out through the gap between the kettle and the steamer.
4. Spread a hemp cloth over the top of the steamer, boil up kettle water until steam comes permeating out of the hemp cloth, and wait for 15 minutes to get the layers of rice powder steamed thoroughly.

Suggestions

- To test to see whether the proper amount of water has been added to the rice powder for moisturizing, hold moistened powder in the palm tightly and shake it over the palm. When the rice powder piece keeps its hardened shape, then the water content is believed to be right. When the rice powder is spread over a redbean layer, do so gently: otherwise the pressed powder will not let steam pass through it, so the rice powder will be ill-steamed. In order to make each layer have uniform thickness, it is better to divide the rice powder equally for each layer in advance.

2. Steamed Bean Cake (*K'ong Siruttŏk*)

Steamed bean cake is made from beans mixed with regular rice flour. It can be steamed as a single homogeneous mass or as layered sheets. In order to give it a little more stickiness, sticker rice flour may be added to it. In the autumn, fresh beans are used, and in the winter, black beans are preferred.

The beans were cultivated at the beginning of the Three Kingdom Period, around the lst Century B. C., and have become the most valuable source of protein and fat of the Korean food. The bean can be used widely in cooked rice and other processed foods such as bean custard, bean paste, soybean sauce, bean powder, bean oil, etc. Besides, in the area of cakes, the bean is used in the steamed bean *siruttŏk*, and other steamed cakes, such as blanched cake, and pounded cake.

These cakes result in supplementing indispensable protein for Koreans. There are several Koran proverbs related to the bean. "Is your bean larger or mine ?" in an argument; "One believes the redbean as the bean when told so." describing a lie; "The bean sprouts out where the bean was planted, while the redbean sprouts out where the redbean was planted," describing a natural result; and "One breaks a large iron kettle while roasting beans," decribing a foolish act-all these seem to suggest that, the bean is closely related to the Korean way of life and food culture. Anyway, since steamed bean cake is easy to make and is also high in protein content, it has been popularly made and enjoyed.

Materials and quantity

rice	15 cups(rice power, 30 cups)
salt	2 Tbsp
water	2 cups
sugar	⅓ cups
fresh beans	6 cups
salt	1 tablespoon

Recipe

1. Wash and soak rice for 12 hours and drain off the water, add salt to it, pounding and sifting it to make fine flour (When devoid of sufficient moisture, spray water over the powder, and rub it with both hands and sift again.).
2. Boil a mixture of water, salt and sugar; cool it and scatter it over the rice flour, rubbing it thoroughly so that the flour is moisturized evenly. Sift it again to get finer rice flour powder.
3. Remove green beans from the pod, wash them and drain off the water completely; add salt to them, and let it permeate into the beans.
4. Mix rice flour and beans.
5. Place the steam screen on the bottom of the steamer and pour the mixture of rice flour and beans. Block the gap between the steamer and the kettle. Cover a wet hemp cloth over the mixture. Steam up and when steam is rising above the mixture, let 15 minutes pass for thorough steaming.

Suggestions

- Water oozes from the salted green beans, which must be drained off, storing the beans on the sift grid before making the mixture.
- This ricecake requires even and strong heat under its kettle for better steaming. About 15 minutes steaming is required for a small steamer, and 30 minutes for a larger steamer, after the first sign of steam over the top of the mixture is observed.

3. Green Pea Cake (*Noktu P'yŏn*)

The green pea cake, *noktu p'yŏn*, is also known as *noktupyŏng*. In the green pea coated steamed cake, *noktu komul siruttŏk*, there are several varieties: they are *chŏmmipyŏng* (粘米餠), *noktu ch'alp'yŏn*, *noktu mesiruttŏk*, *nokmal mesiruttŏk*, *noktu ch'arime siruttŏk*, etc. According to the book published in 1943, the *Chosŏn Mussang Sinsik Yori Chepŏp*(朝鮮 無雙 新式料理 製法), the cooking method of this green pea cake is explained in detail. It says that the green pea cake is made in the following way: first, grind the peas with the grinding stone, and blow off the husks, wash the meat of the peas in fresh water and drain the water. Sift rice flour on a sieve and put it into the steaming utensil, *siru*. One rice flour layer should be around 5 *pun*, *i. e.*, about 15 mm in thickness. The water soaked peas are to be scattered over the rice flour so that the entire surface of the rice flour layer is covered with peas, repeating the same procedure, one layer over another, and sufficient steaming must be done.

The green pea is said to have originated from India and transferred to Korea through China. It is very digestible, has a very high nutritious value and gives off a pleasant fragrance, for which reason it is made into haute quality foods such as green pea gelatin, green pea pancakes(빈대떡), green pea dressing or stuffing, cake decorating or partition powder, green pea tea, and green pea sprouts, all of which are enjoyed as quality foods.

Besides green pea cake, it is used to make green pea gruel, which is also a food of high quality. It is made through the following fashion: first, boil the green peas, mash the blanched green peas, sift them, then let settle, scoop the thin upper layer of green pea liquid and boil it again with soaked rice. When rice is cooked sufficiently becoming enlarged, add the sediment of the green pea to the rice and mix them. Then you can have a very delicious gruel of good quality.

Materials and quantity

glutinous rice	10 cups (its flour 20 cups)	
salt	2 Tbsp	
Mung beans (roughly ground)	6 cups	
salt	2 Tbsp	

Recipe

1. Wash glutinous rice in clean fresh water and let it soak in water for 12 hours, drain off the water, add salt to it, pound it and sift it to get finer glutinous rice powder.
2. Wash and soak skin-peeled green beans in water for 12 hours, and rub them, washing them several times to get rid of any remaining outer crust, and other elements. Steam the green beans in the steamer until they become soft. Sift them through a rough net sieve to make dredging. Steamed green beans may be used without sifting.
3. Place a steam screen on the bottom of the steamer, spread green bean dredging over the screen and then glutinous rice flour about 3 cm thick: their alternating layers are heaped repeatedly, the green bean dredging coming to the top. Then place a wet hemp cloth over the top. Place the steamer over the kettle, and block the gap between the steamer and the kettle with the kneaded steam blocker. The kettle is heated over a strong fire; about 15 minutes are required after the first sign of steam rising from the top of the raw ricecake is observed.

Suggestions

- Green peas should be rubbed thoroughly with both hands so that any remaining skins can be removed completely, and which will help make its dredging color become finer and cleaner.
- Unlike the regular rice powder, glutinous rice flour has the tendency of blocking steam rising through it. Therefore, it is advisable to place a thick dredging layer of green peas in the bottom, on the top of which several layers of regular rice flour with green pea partitioners should be stacked, on which another glutinous rice flour layer may be placed so as to allow steam to rise through the entire mass easily. Regular and glutinous rice flour may be stacked alternately for better steaming effect.

4. Steamed Radish Cake (*Mu Siruttŏk*)

Radish cake is also called *napokpyŏng*(羅蔔餠), whose recipe is given in the work *Puinp'ilji*(Indispensable Information for Ladies), which says, "Slice a radish into thin and broad pieces, soak them in salted water, take them out of the water, and mix them with rice flour. Put the rice flour coated radish slices into the steaming utensil, and those left uncoated may be coated again, putting them over the topmost rice flour layer before final steaming."

The radish cake with redbean layer partitioners is mentioned in the *Kyŭhap Ch'ongsŏ* and the *Imwonsipyukji*, in the latter of which chest-nuts, jujubes, or mugworts are described as being used in the cake.

In the cookbook, the *Hankuk Ttŏk P'yun*, (Korean Cookbook) published in 1986, the recipe of the steamed radish cake is described as follows: Steamed radish cake is made by mixing rice flour with sliced radishes, making the mixture into thick layers and steaming it sufficiently. Anyway, it is the very cake for common people to enjoy.

The radish, which originated from the Mediterranean Sea coasts, is a kind of vegetable whose leaves and roots are edible while its seeds are used as a herbal medicinal drug, and which is also nicknamed as *napuk*(羅蔔). The radish is analyzed to contain the digestive agent diastase together with a lot of vitamin C, which fact reflects that our forefathers were wise enough to introduce and cultivate this vegetable as an indispensable food.

Materials and quantity

Material	Quantity
regular rice	10 cups(rice flour, 20 cups)
salt	2 Tbsp
redbean	6 cups
salt	2 Tbsp
radish	1 kg
sugar	2 Tbsp

Recipe

1. Wash and soak rice in water for 12 hours, drain off the water, add salt, pound and sift it to make finer flour.(When devoid of enough moisture, scatter water over the flour and rub it thoroughly. Sift it again.)
2. Boil redbeans and drain off hot water, pour fresh water over the redbeans, boiling again until the redbeans become soft. Then reduce water and boil again over lukewarm heat to help them mature. Add salt and pound it roughly in the mortar to make dredgings.
3. Slice radish into large pieces, scatter sugar over them and drain off any juicy elements. Mix them with rice flour.
4. Place the steam screen on the bottom of the steamer and put thick redbean dredging over the screen. Form a layer of 4~5 cm thick with the mixture of radish and rice flour. This layer is thicker than that of other ricecakes, then put a layer of redbean dredging over it. This combination of layers is repeated to the brim of the steamer. The steamer is then placed over the kettle and the gap between them should be blocked by paste.
5. Place a wet hemp cloth over the top and put the kettle over high heat. When the first sign of steam is noticed, let 15 minutes elapse. To verify full steaming, pierce a stick into the rice flour layers. When raw rice flour does not come out adhering to the stick, it is a sign that the ricecake is well steamed.

❶

5. Pumpkin Cake (*Hopak Ttŏk*)

The pumpkin cake gives a special flavor compared with other Korean cakes.

Besides regular hopak *ttŏk*, there are *mulhopak ttŏk*, *hopak ch'alttŏk*, *hopak sirup'yŏn*, etc.

In the *Chosŏn Yoripŏp*(Korean Cookery), the cooking methods of *hopak ttŏk* and *mulhopak ttŏk* are mentioned, "*Mulhopak ttŏk* is cooked with sliced pieces of fresh reddish pumpkin which is sweetened with sugar and coated with rice flour. It is then placed in the steaming utensil, *siru*, one layer after another, with redbeans in-between, and then steamed. The glutinous pumpkin cake is made with one-inch long pieces of red pumpkin mixed with rice flour and a sufficient amount of black beans being placed between the layers, and then steamed." Fresh pumpkin cake is different from glutinous pumpkin cake in that the former uses redbeans as a layer partitioner while the latter, chestnut-looking large black beans. The fresh or dried pumpkin has been used in various kinds of dishes: dried sliced pumpkin(*hopak kojari*) for a side dish, dried pumpkin for porridge (*hopak pŏmbŏk*), etc. Fresh pumpkin cake is very palatal because the moisture of the pumpkin mixes well with regular rice flour, giving off a pleasant scent, and a sweet taste particular to the pumpkin itself. The pumpkin is a very important food to Koreans, abundant with carotene which becomes vitamin A in our body and also with indispensable vitamins B and C.

Materials and quantity

rice	10 cups(rice flour, 20 cups)	
salt	½ Tbsp	
boiled sugar solution	1⅓ cups	
(sugar 1 cup, water 2/3 cup)		
fully ripened pumpkin	2 Kg	
salt	½ Tbsp	
redbeans(ground roughly)	4 cups	
salt	1½ Tbsp	

Recipe

1. Wash and soak rice in fresh water for 12 hours, drain off the water, add salt, pound and sift it to get a fine rice powder. Dissolve sugar in water, boil and cool it. Mix it with the rice powder and rub the mixture with hands; sift it again.
2. Peel off the hard cover of a pumpkin, remove its seeds together with its supporting soft tissue, cut it into 4 cm×2 cm pieces, and let them dry in the sun for a couple of days until the skin becomes a little harder.
3. Soak redbeans, rub them several times with the hands and wash them, after each rubbing, in fresh water to remove their outer skins and other foreign elements. Drain off the water completely, steam them until they become soft, add salt and sift them in a rough net sieve.
4. Add sugar to half dried pumpkin pieces, which are then mixed with rice powder, and put the mixture into the steamer before the juice oozes out of them.
5. Place the steam screen on the bottom of the steamer, and spread redbean dredging over it and then the pumpkin and rice powder mix, one after another, alternately. The final layer will be the redbean dredging. Put a wet hemp cloth over it. Put steam blocking paste between the kettle and steamer to prevent any steam from leaking through the gap of the kettle and the steamer. Place the kettle over high heat. When the first sign of steam rises above the hemp cloth, wait for 15 minutes for sufficient steaming.

6. Multi-Fruits Cake (*Chapkwa Pyŏng*)

This cake is made from rice flour mixed with various fruits, and is also called *chapkwa pyŏn* and *chapkwako*.

According to the reference described in the multi-fruits cake section of the cook book, *Ŭmsik Timipang*, "It is made by kneading stickier rice flour; cut it like honey ricecake, *cuak*; blanch it in boiling water and drain water; coat each piece with honey and then dredge with various crushed or sliced dried fruit particles, such as dried persimmons, blanched chestnuts, dried chestnuts, pinenuts, etc." In another reference book, the *Kyuhap Ch'ongsŏ*, published in 1766, the dredging items enumerated are sliced dried jujubes, dried persimmons and sliced fresh chestnuts. In the *Chŭbo Sanrim Kyŏngjae*, the cooking procedure is given in the following fashion: first, soak newly harvested rice in fresh water, then turn it into flour. Prepare boiled fresh chestnuts and jujubes with their seeds removed, and a sliced soft persimmon with its skin peeled off. Mix them with rice flour, and put the mixture into the steaming utensil in several layers with green peas, redbeans or fresh beans as partitioners.

The *Kyuhap Ch'ongsŏ* published in 1815, mentions other multi-fruit cake(*chapkwa-ko/pyŏn* 雜果糕/편), which is the stickier rice fruit cake made from stickier rice and sundry fruits. The book also introduces a new multifruit cake, *shinkwa pyŏng*, (新果餠). It says that this new multi-fruit cake is made by "Preparing blanched chestnuts, sliced chestnuts, mashed fermented persimmon with its crust being peeled off, fresh large beans, and rice flour. Mix them well with honey, covering the entire surface of the steamer with the meat of green beans."

Materials and quantity

regular rice .... 10 cups(rice flour, 20 cups)	dried persimmon ..... 5 ea
salt ..... 2 Tbsp	walnut ..... 10 ea
honey ..... 1 cup	pinenut ..... 2 Tbsp
chestnut ..... 400 g(30 ea)	citron syrup(boiled tangerine skin paste) ..... 1 cup
jujube ..... 100 g(20 ea)	
honey, or brown sugar ..... 2 cups	

Recipe

1. Wash rice and soak it in fresh water for 12 hours, drain off the water, add salt, pound and sift it to get fine rice powder. Pour honey over the rice powder little by little, at the same time stirring and rubbing the powder, first with fingers of one hand, and later with both hands so that they mix thoroughly; sift the mix again to make a powder.
2. Peel off the chestnut's hard crust and inner cover, then slice its meat into 5~6 pieces. The seed of the jujube is removed by peeling off its outer crust, which is cut also into 3~4 pieces. Both the chestnut meat and jujube crust are boiled with sugar. The seeds of dried persimmons are removed and the soft meat is cut into large pieces. The hard shell of the walnuts are crushed to collect the meat. The hard shell of the pinenuts are also removed, and the soft inner coverings are taken off. Sweetened citron crust in syrup is also divided into large blocks.
3. All of these fruit seeds and crusts are put into the rice-honey mix and stirred thoroughly. Then add rice powder to it and mix them sufficiently.
4. The steam screen is placed on the bottom of the steamer and the entire mixture is put over it, placing a wet hemp cloth on its top. Place the steamer over the kettle and put the steam blocker between the steamer and kettle. Place the kettle over strong heat for 15 minutes.

7. White Powder Ricecake (*Paeksŏlki*)

This steamed cake, another kind of traditional *siruttŏk*, has various other nicknames, such as *hwinmuri*, or *k'ongbŏmuri*, or *ssukbŏmuri* according as the bean or mugwort is added. It was documented by the name of *paek sŏlko* in the book, *Kyuhap Ch'ongsŏ*, and has been enjoyed by Koreans for a long time. In another book, *Sŏngosasŏl*, its recipe is given in the following fashion, "Moisten regular rice flour, placing it in the *siru* and steam it sufficiently. It is the basic steamed cake, and for its pure looking color, it is regarded as the purest and cleanest, and is also an indispensable and sacred food of sacrifice to a god or deity."

In the Kyukon Yoram, this paeksŏlki is described as a food of sacrifice in the spring, but as a food of general consumption in the summer. The Korean cookery book, Chosŏn Yoripŏp describes, "Paeksŏlki is made from a mixture of regular rice powder and chestnuts, jujubes, salt, and sugar, forming no layers at all and then steamed in a siru." In another cook book, Chosŏn Yori published in 1940, its recipe is given very simply, "Paeksŏki is made from regular rice flour with some salt added for its seasoning and then by steaming." In the 1958 edition of the Korean cookery book, the Urinara Ŭmsik Mandŭnŭn Pŏp, it is described as a steamed cake hwinmuri, which is made from the mixture of regular and stickier rice flour with sugar, and then steamed.

The white *hwinmuri* is often made for a prayer of well-being and peace, on a new-born baby's third, seventh and one-hundredth survival days; on the first birthday, *tol*, and other birthdays for the reason that this cake is believed to represent purity and chastity because no other cereal is added to the white and clean looking rice powder.

Material and quantity

rice	10 cups(rice powder, 20 cups)
salt	2 Tbsp
sugar	1 cup
water	⅔ cup
honey	2 Tbsp

Recipe

1. Wash rice and soak it in fresh water for 12 hours, drain off water, add salt, pound and sift it to get fine rice powder. If the powder is rather dry, spray water over it and rub it with the hands, sifting it again.
2. Make sugar syrup and scatter it over the rice powder, rub it with hands and sift it again.
3. Place the steam screen on the bottom of the steamer, and then the mixed rice powder. Make the top flat, and put a wet hemp cloth over it. Put the steamer on the kettle, which is then placed on high heat. After the first sign of steam rising above the hemp cloth is noticed, keep on steaming for another 15 minutes.
4. When the cake is well steamed and matured, put the cake on the chopping board and let it cool, and then cut it into several blocks rectangularly, putting each block onto a wooden container or other utensil.

Suggestions

- As every cake requires fine rice flour as its ingredient, this cake is not an exception. Therefore a fine net sieve may be used. It is better to steam the rice powder while it still contains enough moisture.
- Instead of sugar, honey may be used to preserve the freshness of this cake longer.
- When pouring the rice-honey mix into the steamer, it is better to scatter the mix lightly little by little so that air pockets may be formed in the stacked mix, which helps steam to penetrate through the rice flour easily; otherwise, the steam passage may be blocked, as in the case where rice powder is pressed down hard by accident.
- This white ricecake can be dried and used in making gruel for children, or it can be consumed by children as a snack.
- This rice cake is made on the 21st day, 100th day, after birth, 1 year birthday and other birthday celebrations for the reason that its whiteness signifies chastity and prayer for the well-being of the celebrated person.

8. Colored Cake (*Kaksaek P'yŏn*)

The colored cake is a kind of *siru* steamed cake with several layers of colored ingredients and has such varieties as the *paekp'yŏn*, the *sŭngkŏmch'op'yŏn*, and the *kkulp'yŏn*. These colorful cakes are set up on the wedding, the sixtieth birthday celebration tables, and in the other festivities.

The *paekp'yŏn* cake, is made from a mixture of glutinous rice powder and honey juice, which is sifted through a sieve. This moisturized mix is put into a steamer in several layers, with the surface of each layer being decorated with minutely sliced jujubes, boiled chestnuts, stone mushrooms, or pinenuts.

The *kkulpyŏn*, honeyed cake, is prepared in the same fashion as the *paekp'yŏn*. Instead of using white sugar, this cake uses honey and black sugar for coloring, and is also called *kkulsŏlki*.

The *sŭngkŭmch'opyŏn* is the same in the cooking method, but dried angelica leaves are added, giving it a particular flavor and taste.

Materials and quantity

White ricecake

- rice .... 5 cups (powder, 10 cups)
- salt .... ½ Tbsp
- sugar .... 1 cup
- water .... ⅔ cup
- chestnut .... 5 ea
- jujube .... 7 ea
- stone mushroom . 3 ea
- pinenut .... 1 Tbsp

Honey cake

- rice .... 5 cups (powder, 10 cups)
- salt .... ½ Tbsp
- honey .... ½ cup
- brown sugar .... ½ cup
- water .... ⅓ cup
- aged soybean sauce .... 1 Tbsp

Angelica cake

- rice .... 5 cups (powder, 10 cups)
- salt .... ½ Tbsp
- angelica powder .... 2½ Tbsp
- sugar .... 1 cup
- water .... ⅔ cup
- chestnut .... 5 ea
- jujube .... 7 ea
- stone mushroom .... 3 pieces
- pinenut ...... 1 Tbsp

Recipe

1. Wash rice and soak it in water for 12 hours, drain off the water, add salt, pound and sift it to get fine flour(powder).
   For white cake, sugar syrup is boiled and let cool. Mix the rice powder with sugar syrup and rub the mix with the hands, and sift it again.
2. For honey cake, boil brown sugar syrup and let it cool, to which aged soybean sauce and honey are added. Rub the mix with both hands. For angelica cake, mix angelica powder with rice flour. The remaining process is the same as that of white cake.
3. For garnishing, slice the chestnut, jujube, stone mushroom. Cut jujubes into two pieces in the middle.
4. Place the steam pad in the bottom of the steamer. Put honey cake mix 2 cm thick, over which garnishing will be poured. A sheet of oiled paper is placed over the garnishing, and other types of cake materials, such as, white cake and angelica cake powders, are stacked in the same fashion. And on the top, a wet hemp cloth will be placed as a cover. Put the steamer on the kettle, glue the gap between the steamer and kettle with rice flour paste. The kettle is to be put over high heat. After the first sign of steam rising over the hemp cloth, a period of 30~40 minutes is required for fully steamed cooking.

9. Multi-Colored Cake *(Ssaek Ttŏk,* or Rainbow Cake *Mujigie Ttŏk)*

This one block steamed ricecake with no other ingredients added, is called *musuri ttŏk.* The *ssaek ttŏk* is made with multi- colored rice flour layers stacked one colored layer after another without placing any partitioners in-between. Instead, sweetened water is sprinkled over each layer for moistening so that better steaming effects can be attained.

Recently, some people use edible color additives, angelica leaves, cocoa powder to dye the rice flour beautifully by sifting the mixture with a sieve, but traditionally natural coloring agents have been used: for the yellow color, gardenia seeds are pounded, immersed and soaked in water, and then removed, and the remaining colored liquid is added to rice flour to make the dough; for the blue color, mugwort liquid; for the red color, *omija,* Schizandra chinensis, and for the red color, *yŏnji,* a coloring agent for rouge.

These coloring additives have an abundant amount of good nutrients: the mugwort has bountiful minerals and vitamin C which are good for preventing a cold, and the Schizandra chinensis has the effect of activating physiological functions of the body. On the other hand, cocoa is analyzed as having a lot of calcium, iron, and potassium contents, which are good sources of minerals necessary for the child and the aged to maintain their health, and also helpful in the recuperation from fatigue of mountain climbing and hard physical activities.

The steamed cake, *mujigettŏk,* rainbow cake, is very colorful to look at, and also delicious to the palate.

Materials and quantity

rice .... 8 cups(rice powder, 16 cups)
glutinous rice .. 2 cups(rice powder, 4 cups)
salt .... 2 Tbsp
sugar .... 2 cups

cinnamon powder(or cocoa powder) ... 3 Tbsp
gardenia seed .... 2 pieces
(yellow food coloring additive, a little)
omija, five-flavor seed .... 50 g
(red food coloring additive, a little)

Recipe

1. Wash regular and glutinous rice in fresh water, mix them and soak the mixture for 12 hours, drain off the water, add salt and pound it, add sugar and sift it to get a fine rice powder. Divide it into five portions.
2. Wash fresh mugwort, and dry it sufficiently. Make its powder in a mixer. Soak gardenia and *omija* seeds until their dark colors of yellow and red are oozed out.
3. Add 4 different colors of additives to the four portions of rice flour, except one for the white. Spray water over each colored portion, rub and sift each to get fine colored flour. The right amount of moisture of the flour can be tested by gripping a small amount of it in the palm. If the condensed powder remains rather intact when it is swayed on the open palm, we can say it contains the right amount of moisture.
4. Put the steam screen on the bottom of the steamer, place each colored rice powder one by one to make five colored layers. Put the steam blocker between the steamer and kettle. Then put a wet hemp cloth over the top of the steamer. Place the kettle over high heat. After the first sign of steam rising above the hemp cloth, let 15 more minutes pass for full steam cooking. Instead of cutting the cake, turn over the steamer and let the cake fall on a flat surface. Proper dredging may be used for decoration, and beautiful candle sticks may be planted on the top to make it a fine birthday celebration ricecake.

10. Pine Cake (*Songp'yŏn*)

Songp'yŏn is also called *songpyŏng*, and is similar to *cholp'yŏn* in that they use the same material, that is, rice. But the method of making *songp'yŏn* is unique. First of all, regular rice powder is kneaded with hot water, and by making a hollow space in the dough with a thumb to put stuffings in it, a half moon shaped cake is finally formed for steaming. Then each piece is placed in a steamer over pine needles, stacking one layer after another in the same fashion. This cake is made and enjoyed all over the country, especially on the occasion of the August Moon Festival, *ch'usŏk*, when *songp'yŏn* is made from newly harvested cereals. This pine cake is made in various colors so that different names are given according to their colors: the white one is *hwin songp'yŏn*; the green one, *ssuk songp'yŏn* (mixed with mugwort); the brown one, *songgi songp'yŏn*(mixed with pine's inner soft crust, endodermis).

Another variety of names are given to this cake according to what kind of stuffings are used. The stuffing materials are redbeans, black beans, fresh beans, green peas, chestnuts, jujubes, sesame, (green) perilla seeds, etc. These are used with their hulls or husks peeled off.

Therefore we can have *p'atsongp'yŏn*(redbean pine cake), *p'utk'ong songpyŏn*(fresh bean pine cake) and the like. The size of the pine cake also varies according to the region. Usually, a large size is preferred in the northern region, whereas a smaller one is adopted in Seoul.

Before *ch'usŏk*, fine and soft pine needles are gathered and washed in clean water and trimmed very neatly, which are used to cover this stuffed ricecake one layer after another so that they eventually stick to the ricecake, which leaves their needle prints on the cake and scent of fresh pine so that the enduring scent of the pine mixes with the stickiness of the crust of rice, and flavor of the stuffing, and all these combine to give a special flavor and taste of this Korean ricecake.

Materials and quantity

rice	5 cups(rice powder, 10 cups)
salt	1 Tbsp
chestnut	200 g(10 ea)
sugar	2 Tbsp
mugwort 50 g,	salt ¼ tsp
color additive(yellow, red)	¼ tsp
fresh bean 100 g,	salt ¼ tsp
sesame 100 g,	honey 3 Tbsp
redbean(roughly ground)/green bean	1 cup
honey 5 Tbsp,	salt ½ tsp
cinnamon powder	1 Tbsp
pine leaves	300 g
sesame oil	several drops

Recipe

1. Wash and soak rice for 12 hours, drain off the water, add salt, pound and sift it to obtain fine rice flour. Poach mugwort in boiling water with salt added, wait until its color turns greener, and pound it in a mortar.
2. Divide the rice powder into three portions. Add pounded mugwort to one portion and pound again in a mortar. Add a color additive and boiling water to another portion of the rice powder, and knead it thoroughly until the dough becomes very soft.
3. Peel off the hard crust of chestnuts, cut each into 3~4 pieces, add sugar to it and boil it lightly. Remove fresh beans out of their husks, and add salt. Wash sesame, drain off the water, sear, and put honey into it. Remove the outer skin from the soaked redbeans, boil them in water, and pound them in the mortar. Add salt, honey and cinnamon.
4. Detach a small piece from the dough of ②, and with the thumb make a hollow space in the center, put the stuffing of ③ into the space, put the edges together and press it with the fingers of both hands to give it a trim shape.
5. Spread pine leaves over the bottom of the steamer and then put pine cake over the leaves. Spread pine leaves over the raw pine cake to make another layer and so forth. When the first sign of steam is noticed on the top, cover the steamer for sufficient steaming. When well steamed, remove the pine leaves and soak and wash the pieces of cake in cool fresh water. Remove cake pieces from the water and apply sesame oil to them.

11. Thick Cake (*Tut'ŏp Ttŏk*)

The name of this thick cake is derived from its form, for its ingredients are heaped as a half ball in the steaming vessel, *siru*, before steaming, and it is easy to remove each hemispherical cake from the steamer with a bowl by scooping.

It is nicknamed *hondobyŏng* or *hapbyŏng*, which, for its half ball shape, can be contained in a bowl almost fully and completely like a cup cake. Since the cake can be contained in a bowl naturally, and eaten as a whole rather than being cut into pieces before serving, it must have picked up the name *hapbyŏng*, an equal shape cake. This cake was highly valued in the royal palace and was indispensable at the king's birthday celebration. Its covering is made with redbeans whose husks are removed first, then seared in a fry pan so that its taste and flavor become enticing. On the other hand, the stuffing is composed of honeyed redbeans, jujubes, pinenuts, citrons, etc., so that the stuffing gives a particular look and taste to the cake.

This *tut'ŏp ttŏk* is basically a glutinous rice-cake. Rice is boiled or steamed, and then sifted with a coarse sieve, to make minute particles. These rice flour particles are heaped hither and thither, like a half ball in the vessel, over the dredging. Stuffing is then studded into the rice flour ball, covering the entire surface with dredging to form a flat and uniform level, and then final steaming is done. Its dredging is different from others in flavor and taste although the same material may be used. A different way of stacking can be done like this: the stickier rice flour is scooped with a spoon to make half balls, where stuffing is inserted, and redbean dredging covers the layer, and final steaming is carried out.

Recipe

1. Wash and soak glutinous rice for 12 hours, drain off water, add salt, pound it, and sift it to obtain a fine powder. Add aged soybean sauce and honey, rub the mix with the hands, and sift again.
2. Wash roughly ground redbeans in water, rub them to get rid of their outer crust, put them into a steamer, and steam them. Then sift them through a rough net sieve while they are still warm, and add aged soybean sauce, white sugar, and brown sugar to them, and fry them in a fry pan to the extent they become dryish. Sift them again through a rough grid sieve.
3. To make stuffing, trim the chestnuts and jujubes and mince them.

   Mince citron crust in syrup, and trim the pinenuts. Mix the seared redbeans with honey, minced citron, and cinnamon powder, knead the mix, and detach a chestnut size dough from the mix. Insert the chestnut, jujube and pinenut to the detached dough, and make it flat and round.
4. Spread a hemp cloth on the bottom of the steamer, and spread the redbean dredging over it. Place glutinous rice powder mounds separately over the redbean layer. Put chestnut size dough pieces decorated with the chestnut, jujube and pinenut over the top of the glutinous rice mounds, and then cover the top with another scoop of the glutinous rice powder. Put one more layer of the redbeans over them. The next mound will be made on the valley of the previous layer. Thus, three or four more layers of mounds and redbeans will be stacked. Steam them and after the first sign of steam rising above the top layer, leave it 15~20 more minutes for full steaming.

Materials and quantity

glutinous rice		5 cups(powder, 10 cups)
aged soybean sauce		3 Tbsp
honey syrup	honey	⅔ cup
	water	½ cup

redbean dredging

redbean(roughly ground)	8 cups
aged soybean sauce	4 Tbsp
white sugar	2 cups
cinnamon powder	2 tsps
black pepper	a small quantity

stuffing

seared redbean	2 cups,	citron syrup	2 Tbsp
honey	2 Tbsp,	chestnut	10 ea
jujube	10 ea,	pinenut	1 Tbsp
cinnamon powder	½ Tbsp		

12. Fermented Ricecake (*Chŭngp'yŏn*)

C hŭngp'ŏn is made with fermented rice dough, which is placed into a frame, with garnishing jujubes, pinenuts, manna lichens, i.e., stone mushrooms, etc., which are spread over the surface of the cake layer. It is called by various names according to regional differences, such as *kichuttŏk*, *kichŭngpyŏng*, *kichittŏk*, *sulttŏk*, and *pŏnggŏjittŏk*. Its freshness can be preserved a little longer, compared with other cakes, due to the fact that it is fermented with undistilled liquor. Therefore, it is more favored during the summer season.

Its recipe is given in several books in detail, the *Ŭmsik Timipang*, *Kyuhap Ch'ongsŏ*, and *Kanp'yŏn Chosŭn Yori Chepŏp*, but their recipes differ in detail. According to the *Ŭmsik Timipang*, quality rice is first soaked in liquor, and then placed in a steaming vessel and cooked like frost flower cake, *sangwhapyŏng*. In the *Chupangmun*, the layer partitioner is placed one layer after another. In the *Yorok* and the *18 Segi Kungjung Yŏnhwae Umsik Ko* various garnishings are enumerated, such as chestnuts, jujubes, and pinenuts. And in the *Kyuhap Ch'onsŏ*, *Puinp'ilji and Siŭijŏnsŏ*, besides nuts, angelica, stone mushrooms, cinnamon, dried ginger powder, and pepper are listed as being favored garnishings.

In the *Kyuhap Chonsŏ*, and the *Siŭi Chunsŏ*, redbeans and sesame seeds are recommend for dressing. Instead of undistilled liquor, the sweet drink, *kamju*, is recommended, while in the *Tongguk Sesigi*, glutinous rice is preferred.

Material and quantity

rice .... 5 cups(powder 10 cups)
salt .... ½ Tbsp
makkŏlli(unstrained rice wine) .. 2 cups
sugar .... ½ cup
boiling water .... ½ cup
jujube .... 10 ea
stone mushroom .... 8 pieces
pinenut .... 1 Tbsp

Recipe

1. Wash and soak rice in water for 12 hours, drain off the water, add salt, pound and sift it several times to obtain fine flour.
2. Wipe off any dust from the jujube, peel off its crust lengthwise, and slice it. Soak the stone mushroom, wash it by rubbing it with the hands, wipe off water and slice it.
3. Add sugar and indirectly heated liquor *makkŏlli* to one-half of the rice powder and knead it. Add boiling water to the remaining one-half of the rice powder and knead it. Mix the two kinds of dough and knead and pound it for a long time.
4. Put the mixed dough in a ceramic container and cover it with a thick lid, and place it in a warm place for fermenting for 3~4 hours. When the dough becomes inflated, pound it with a long round wooden bar and, leave it for another 1~2 hours for further fermenting.
5. After allowing it to inflate three times, place a hemp cloth on the bottom of a steamer, put the fermented dough over the hemp cloth, about 2~3 cm thick, and decorate it with jujubes, and stone mushrooms. Steam it for 20~30 minutes over high heat. The final cake form is round and flat.

13. Honeyed Ricecake (*Yaksik*)

Yaksik, or *yakpap* is a glutinous ricecake, which is one of the most favored desserts-a must to be set up on the table of festivity. The cake was originally a concentrated dietal food to be served on the first full-moon day of the new year, that is, January 15 by the lunar calendar.

According to a Korean history book, the *Samkook Yusa*(三國遺事), the origin of this cake is described like this: the 21st king of the Shilla Kingdom, King Soji, after ten years' reign, was informed by a crow of a coming catastrophe so that he could prepare and save his life. The king ordered that *yaksik* be cooked to offer to the crows as a sign of gratitude to the spirit of the life-saver crow. This custom of preparing *yaksik* has been handed down to the present so it is quite common to observe that it is prepared all over the country for festivities, especially as a dietal food on January 15.

The meaning of *yak* in *yaksik*, is two-fold: one is 'medicine' for curing diseases, and the other, 'beneficial', and therefore *yaksik* signifies a good food. In Korea, honey is called *yak*: as a result, honey wine is called *yakju*; honeyed rice, *yakpap*; and honeyed fruit, *yakkwa*. The *yaksik* is brownish in color, oily in appearance and savory in taste. As to the recipe of *yaksik*, the *Yŏlyang Sesigi* made public in 1819, says, "Steam glutinous rice until finally cooked, add sesame oil, honey, concentrated soybean sauce, seedless jujubes, and sliced chestnuts onto it, and then steam the entire concoction thoroughly to make very delicious *yakpap* ready to be served."

Materials and quantity

glutinous rice	5 cups
salt	½ Tbsp
chestnut	10 ea
jujube	10 ea
white sugar	½ cup
brown sugar	1 cup
cinnamon powder	1 tsp
jujube seed(for extraction by boiling)	3 Tbsp
caramel sauce	3 Tbsp
honey	⅓ cup
sesame oil	2 Tbsp

How to make caramel sauce

- **Materials**: 6 Tbsp of sugar, 3 Tbsp of fresh water, 3 Tbsp of boiled water.

- **Recipe**: Put sugar and fresh water into a pan and boil until large air pockets are formed, and the edge of the mix begins to burn, then lower the heat, and stir thoroughly with a fla t wooden spoon. When the mixture turns bro wn, then add boiled water and mix it well le st it should stick to the pan.

Recipe

1. Wash glutinous rice, soak for 12 hours, and drain off the water. Place a hemp cloth on the bottom of the steamer, pour rice into it, and steam it for one hour. When steam starts to rise, scatter salted water over the rice and stir thoroughly with a flat wooden spoon and then steam it again.
2. Peel off the hard crust of the chestnuts, and cut each into two or three pieces lengthwise.
3. Trim the jujubes, wash them, remove their seeds and cut them into three parts lengthwise. Boil the jujube seeds in water and sift its extracted juice. Trim the pinenuts, removing their soft inner skin.
4. While the steamed glutinous rice is still hot, remove it to a large container, spread it and add to it sugar, cinnamon power, aged soybean sauce, the jujube seed juice, caramel sauce, honey, and sesame oil, and mix them well. Add once more sesame oil, chestnuts, jujubes and pinenuts and mix them well.
5. Put the mix into the steamer and heat it indirectly in boiling water, first over high heat, then lower heat for 8 hours.

1. Sticky Ricecake (*Injŏlmi*)

*I*njŏlmi is a popular ricecake next to the steamed *siru ttŏk*. Both *injŏlmi* and *cŏlp'yŏn* are made in the same way, but the materials are different, the *injŏlmi* using stickier rice, whereas *cŏlp'yŏn*, regular rice. These types of cake are made from steamed rice powder, which is later pounded on a flat wood block board with a wooden hammer or in a mortar with a wooden pestle. Cooked glutinous rice can be used directly without being powdered. It is given several names, such as, *injŏlpyŏng* (印切餠), a homophonous *injŏlpyŏng*(引切餠), or *injŏlmi*(引截米). The cake pounded on the flat board with a wooden hammer is more delicious and chewy than the one made in the mortar. In several books, the recipe of *injŏlmi* is mentioned. The *Chŭngbo Sanrim Kyŏngje*, (Revised Forestry Economics), and the *Imwon Sipyukji* describe *injŏlmi* as a ricecake dredged with seared bean powder, while the *Sŭngho Sasŏl*, the recipe is given in the following way: the base of the cake is prepared from glutinous rice and pounded on a wooden board with wooden hammers, to which seared bean powder is dredged. This must be the oldest written record of the present day *injŏlmi*.

In the *Urinara Ŭmsik Mantŭnŭn Pŏp*(Korean Cookery), the cake is listed by various names besides the *injŏlmi*, such as *pat' injŏlmi*, *k'ongkaru injŏlmi*, *kkae injŏlmi*, *ssuk injŏlmi*, *taech'u injŏlmi*, etc., according to the material used as dredging. The reason that *injŏlmi* is nicknamed *injŏlpyŏng*, literally meaning 'pulling cut cake', is that the cake shrinks but is eventually cut off when pulled from two opposite ends.

Materials and quantity

glutinous rice ..... 10 cups(powder, 20 cups)
salt .... 2 Tbsp
water .... ½ cup

dredging

yellow bean powder .... 1 cup
green bean powder .... 1 cup
sugar .... 1 Tbsp
black perilla .... 1 cup

Recipe

1. Wash and soak glutinous rice for more than 12 hours, drain off water, and put it into a steamer. Steam it over high heat until it is almost cooked. Make salt water and spray it into the half-cooked glutinous rice, and steam it again for thorough steaming.
2. Season three kinds of dredging with sugar.
3. Pound the well-steamed glutinous rice in a mortar. Coat salted water over the pestle for a better pounding effect.
4. The pounded glutinous rice dough is then spread with a round wooden ladle over a flat wood board, cut into pieces about the size of 3 cm by 5 cm.
5. Each piece is coated with three different kinds of dredgings: yellow and green bean powder, and black perilla.

Suggestions

- Instead of glutinous rice, which takes time and effort to knead into dough by pounding, glutinous rice powder may be used for effective steaming and for better tasty dough.
- When pounding an ingredient in a mortar, pound it hard and coat often the pestle with salt water, so that air pockets may be formed in the dough. When pounding on a flat wooden board, the pounder should be pushed forward after each stroke for easier removal of the pounder from the sticky dough. *Injŏlmi* becomes tasty when it contains the right amount of salt.

2. Thimble Cake and Flower Cake (*Kolmu Ttŏk* and *Kkot Chŏlp'yŏn*)

Koreans hold the *kosa* ceremony, dedicating the *siru* cake and a bowl of fresh water as sacrifices to a deity or spirits of the house on the last day of the year, and also prepare the white cake *hwin ttŏk* in the shape of a thimble to share with neighbors. The book *Siŭi Pang* has a description about thimble cake, a thin-sliced ricecake, "It is made by pounding the steamed rice dough, which is rolled into a finger thick shape and then cut into a piece of about the size of 5 cm long. These little block pieces are pressed onto various patterns of molds and then oiled thereafter."

The *chŏlp'yŏn* belongs to the category of non-steamed cake, and means white cake cut off from the mass. This cake is classified according to its dying material to be used and its ingredients to be mixed: moon-shaped *tal ttŏk*, a round shape cake in various colors, a dragon shaped *yongttŏk*, a bird shaped *saettŏk*, a bird shaped colored *saekttŏk*, a silk worm shaped *koch'i ttŏk*, etc. There are *ssuk chŏlp'yŏn*, and *songki chŏlp'yŏn*, which are similar to the white cake, and prepared on a new year's day, and mixed with wormwood and pine endodermis, respectively. There is also *sulich'a chŏlp'yŏn* prepared on May 5, *tano-nal*, which has an imprint of a cart wheel on it.

Chŏlp'yŏn is set up on the large wedding ceremonial table. On the other hand, the flower cake is made from *chŏlp'yŏn*, and on the flat surface of its round shape, flower pedals are placed for decoration.

Materials and quantity

rice .... 10 cups(powder, 20 cups)
salt .... 2 Tbsp
parboiled mugwort .... 50 g
red and blue coloring additives .. a small quantity
sesame oil .... a small quantity

Recipe

1. Wash and soak rice for 12 hours, drain off the water, add salt, then pound and sift it to obtain a fine powder. When the powder is rather dry, then spray it with water, rub it with both hands, and sift it again.
2. Scatter water over the rice powder to the degree of dryishness and stir thoroughly, with a care not to make the powder too wet as to form a sticky mass. Steam the powder and pound it hard in a mortar to the point where air foams are formed in the dough. For white cake, about 1/2 of the rice powder may be used, often coating the pestle with salt water.
3. To make mugwort flower cake, parboil the mugwort in salt water, wash it and drain off the water. Put it in a mortar with the other half of the steamed rice powder, and pound the mix hard until air foams are noticed.
4. To make thimble cake, roll the pounded dough on a flat wooden board, then cut a roll into pieces with one hand instead of a knife while rolling it gently with the other hand, i. e., into the dough of 4~5 cm long and with two tails on both ends.
5. To make flower cake, put red, yellow or mugwort rice balls over each thimble cake and press them with a patterned wood mould.

3. Wind Cake *(Kaep'i Ttŏk)*

K*aep'i ttŏk* is in the shape of a half moon stuffed with green pea paste and air, from which its nickname *param ttŏk* is derived. Its crust is made from *cŏlp'yŏn*, cut cake, mixed with other coloring elements, such as wormwood for green, or pine endodermis for pink.

These days it is difficult to obtain pine endodermis, so artificial coloring elements are used, instead. The wind cake is made from steamed rice powder, *sŏlki*, for *chŏlp'yŏn*, to which a coloring element is added, and then pounded in a mortar.

Then the pounded *sŏlki* is flattened to make the round crust.

A spoonful of stuffing is put in the center and the two extreme sides are put together to make a bulged half moon shape, leaving a space filled with air beside the stuffing. Stuffing is usually made from redbean paste.

This is what the *Cosŏn Yori*, Korean Cookery, describes as *kap'i ttŏk*(加皮餅).

This inflated cake looks very delicious and pretty for its bulged shape, containing redbean stuffing.

The cake is usually made in the spring when new and fresh wormwood and its shoots are available.

Materials and quantity

- rice .... 5 cups(powder, 10 cups)
- salt .... 1 Tbsp
- mugwort .... 50 g
- salt .... 1/4 tsp

stuffing

- redbean(roughly ground) . 2 cups
- salt .... 1/2 cup
- honey, or sugar 1/3 or 1/2 cup
- cinnamon powder .... 1 Tbsp

sesame oil .... a small quantity

Recipe

1. Wash and soak rice for 12 hours, drain off the water, add salt, pound and sift to obtain fine flour. If the flour powder is too dry, spray water over it and rub with the hands and sift again.
2. Scatter boiling water over the rice powder and stir, then put it into the steamer for steaming. Put the steamed rice powder into a mortar and pound, until air foam is noticed, to make a sticky dough mass.
3. To make mugwort wind cake, *ssuk kaepittŏk*, preboil the mugwort in salted water, wash and drain off the water. Pound it in a mortar and mix with the steamed rice powder to make green cake pieces.
4. Wash the redbean and rub off its crust in water. Boil it in salted water, and drain. Add another scoop of fresh water in the redbean and boil it again until it becomes completely soft. Then lower the heat for maturing. Drain off the water and knead it with a flat wooden spoon and sift. Add salt, honey and cinnamon powder to the sifted redbeans and make small balls of stuffing out of the redbean mass.
5. Put the rice cake dough on a flat wood board and roll it flat with a wooden roller. Put small ball stuffing over the flat dough, fold it and press half circle edges together. Then cut the stuffed portion off by pressing a hallow cylinder object, or a bowl over it.

4. Dredged Rice Ball Cakes—I
(Chestnut *Pam Tanja*, Wugwort *Ssuk Tanja*, Stone Mushroom *Sŏki Tanja*)

There are many kinds of dredged rice balls, such as chestnut, wormwood, and stone mushroom balls, etc. *Tanja* is basically the same in its contents as *injŏlmi*, although its size is smaller. It is used as a decorating element of the multi-colored cakes. It is more colorful in a sense than *kyŏngdan* because it uses many different materials as its auxiliary ingredients, and its dredging materials are gorgeous.

Tanja must have a covering for dredging, which must match with the mix added to the rice base. The wormwood mix must be harmonious with the redbeam dredging; chestnuts, with chestnut dredging; stone mushroom, with pinenut dredging; and jujubes, with jujube dredging, whereby they help each other to make the *tanja* more savory and tasteful.

The names of its varieties are determined by the material used as a mix. They are *taech'u tanja* with jujubes; *ŭnhaeng tanja* with gingko seed; *sŏki tanja* with stone mushrooms; *kamja tanja* with potatoes; *yulmu tanja* with Job's tears; *ssukkuri tanja* with mugwort; *yuja tanja* with citron, etc.

The *pam tanja* first appeared in the *Sul Mantŭnŭn Pŏp*, (Brewing Method), published between 1700 and 1800, where the *tanja* is described to be made from kneading glutinous rice powder, and around the outer surface of the ball, boiled chestnut particles are dredged. With regard to the cookery of *ssukkuli tanja*, the *Chŭngbo Sanrim Kyŏngje*, published in 1766, named it as *hyangae tanja*, which is made from glutinous rice flour, and soft fragrant mugwort, to which honey and chestnuts are added as stuffing. The *sŏki tanja* was first recorded in the *Kunhak Whedong*, made public during the 1800s, and described in *Chosŭn Yori Pŏp* of 1938 where its recipe is given, "Stone mushrooms are minced finely, to which rice flour is added to make a mixture. Coarse pinenut powder is used for its dredging."

Materials and quantity

Chestnut tanja

- glutinous rice .. 3 cups (rice flour, 6 cups)
- salt .... ½ Tbsp

chestnut .... 800 g

stuffing

- mashed chestnut 1 cup
- citron syrup .... 1 Tbsp
- salt .... ⅛ Tbsp
- sugar .... 1 Tbsp
- honey .... 1 Tbsp
- cinnamon powder .... ½ Tbsp

honey .... ½ cup

mugwort tanja

- glutinous rice .. 3 cups (powder, 6 cups)
- salt .... ½ Tbsp
- preboiled mugwort 40 g, or mugwort powder .... 3 Tbsp
- salt .... ¼ tsp

stuffing

- jujube .... 10 ea
- citron syrup ...... 2 Tbsp
- honey .... 2 Tbsp

honey .... ½ cup

Stone much room tanja

- glutinous rice .... 3 cups (powder, 6 cups)
- salt .... ½ Tbsp

stone mushroom powder .... 3 Tbsp

honey .... ½ cup

shredded pinenut ... 1 cup

Recipe

Chestnut *tanja*

1. Add water to and knead the glutinous rice powder to make the dough dryish. Spread a hemp cloth on the bottom of the steamer, put the dough over it and have it fully steamed. Remove the steamed dough into a large container and stir until air foam is formed in the dough.
2. Boil the peeled chestnuts, and pound and sift them. Add about 1 cup of the minced citron in syrup, salt, sugar, honey, and cinnamon powder and mix them well to make stuffing.
3. Apply honey to the hands, detach a chestnut size piece of dough, and put the stuffing in the center, make it round and apply honey over it. Then cover it with chestnut dredging when serving.

Mugwort *tanja*

1. Detach large blocks out of it, and put them into the steamer for steaming. Boil the green mugwort in salted water, and drain. Put them into a mortar and pound hard so that the green color of the mugwort is evenly spread.
2. Mince citron crust in syrup, peel off the crust of jujube lengthwise, add honey to them and mix so that the stuffing is ready.
3. The next steps are the same as in chestnut *tanja3.*

Stone mushroom *tanja*

1. Soak the stone mushroom in hot water, rub it with hands, and wash it in fresh water. Trim it, let it dry in the sun, and pound in a mortar to make it into a powder.
2. Mix the glutinous rice powder with the stone mushroom powder, add water to the mix and knead it to make a large, thick and flat block. Place a hemp cloth on the bottom of the steamer, put the dough block over it, and steam sufficiently.
3. Then remove the steamed block into another container and stir until air foams are formed.
4. Apply honey to the chopping board, transfer the steamed block onto it and flatten into about 1 cm thick. Let it cool, and cut out pieces of 3 cm × 2. 5 cm, to which honey is applied.

   It is then dredged with shredded pinenuts.

5. Dredged Rice Ball Cakes — II

(Multi-Color *Saek Tanja*, Gingko *Ŭnhaeng Tanja*, Jujube *Taech'u Tanja*)

The usual shape of this dredged rice ball is round, but there are exceptions. It is not a seasonal festive cake, but a decoration element put on various main and independent cakes. *Tanja* is the name used in the royal palaces, while *kyŏngtan*, among the folks, having various names depending on the kind of mixes added to the rice base.

Season-wise, mugwort rice balls with stuffing are made in the spring, chestnut balls in the autumn, and jujubes, stone mushroom, and mugwort balls in the winter. However, jujubes and stone mushroom *tanja*, and mugwort *tanja* with stuffing-all these are made throughout a year.

The ginkgo balls are prepared mainly in the palaces, whose ingredients are listed as glutinous rice flour, ginkgo, honey, pinenuts, and salt in the *Chosŏn Yori* (Korean Dishes) of 1940. The materials for the jujube ball are given as jujubes, glutinous rice flour, pinenuts, honey, etc., in the *Cosŏn Yori Pop*, 'Korean Cookery' of 1938.

The *tanja* has many varieties depending upon its cookery. But as a food of time-worn customs, it is an indispensable cake on a baby's first birth day, and also a popular and traditional Korean food enjoyed all the year round.

Materials and quantity

glutinous rice (powder, 15 cups)	7 cups
salt	1½ Tbsp
ginkgo(shredded)	1 cup
jujube	10 ea
dredging	
chestnut	300 g(15 ea)
jujube	100 g(20 ea)
stone mushroom	10 g
stuffing	
jujube	100 g(20 ea)
citron syrup	⅓ cup
cinnamon powder	¼ tsp
shredded pinenut	1 cup
honey	1 cup

Recipe

1. Wash and soak glutinous rice for 12 hours, drain off the water, then add salt, and pound and sift it to obtain a fine powder, which is then divided into three portions.
2. Put the shredded ginkgo into a portion, and minced jujube into another. A third portion is left intact.
3. For colored *tanja*, first of all, peel off the crust of the jujubes lengthwise and mince them, then peel off the hard crust of the chestnuts and shred them. Trim the stone mushroom. Steam these three items for a while, and make each material dredging.
4. Stuffing is concocted by using shredded jujubes, sweetened citron crust, and cinnamon powder. Make a round ball with the stuffing mix, about the size of a ginkgo seed.
5. Spread a wet hemp cloth, on which the three kinds of dredging are placed separately. After steaming, each portion is put into three containers separately and stirred until air foams are formed in them.
6. Apply honey over the chopping board, put ginkgo *tanja* dough on it, and roll it to the thickness of 1 cm. After chilling it for a while, cut it off into a ball 3 cm × 2. 5 cm in size. Apply honey over the ball and then shredded pinenuts over the honeyed surface for ordinany *tanja*. For colored *tanja*, shredded chestnuts are used for white, jujubes for red and the stone mushroom for black. They are applied over the honeyed surface. Add shredded pinenuts to each colored *tanja*.

1. Azalea Flower Cake (*Chintalrae Whajŏn*) **Chijinun Ttok**

W*hajŏn* is a special cake which expresses adequately the coming of a new season by decorating, on its topside, blooming flower petals or the leaves of a flower stem in season. In the spring, the petals of azalea flowers are used on the cake to decorate its surface beautifully: in summer, yellow rose leaves; in the fall, the mother of chrysanthemum leaves. This cake was first mentioned in the *Tomun Taejak* as *chŏnwha pŏp*(煎花法) and *yujŏn pyŏng*(油煎餠), and it was also mentioned equally in the *Umsik Timipang* as *chŏnwha pŏp*.

In the *Ŭmsik Timipang* and *Chupang Mun*, a mixture of glutinous rice and buckwheat is prescribed to be used, whereas in the *Chŭnbo Sanrim Kyŏngjae*, only glutinous rice flour is recommended.

In relation to the Korean traditional customs, our forefathers seemed to try to adapt themselves to nature and also endeavor to be harmonious with nature by preparing food with natural herbal ingredients. Representative examples can be found in the picnic for enjoying flowers, *kkotnori* (花柳) and in prepa-ring the pancake *kkot jŏn* (花煎) with flower petals decorated at the event.

On March 3 by the lunar calendar, *samjit-nal*, folks went out to a hill or valley for a picnic, where azalea flowers were in full bloom. Males held arrow shooting tournaments, while females cooked this round and flat pan-fry cake with azelea petals they had gathered, using at the same time sesame seed oil. In the royal palaces, on this day, the king and his entourage went out to the secret garden of the palace to have a *whajŏn nori*, a feast of flower-fried cakes with azalea flower petals.

Materials and quantity

glutinous rice (powder, 10 cups)	5 cups
salt	½ Tbsp
hot water	1 cup
azalea flower blossom	10 ea
jujube	10 ea
crown daisy	50 g
honey or sugar syrup	½ cup
vegetable oil	1 cup

Recipe

1. Wash and soak glutinous rice for 12 hours, drain off the water, add salt, pound and sift it to obtain fine rice flour.
2. Knead the rice flour with hot water, and make round and flat pieces of about 5 cm in diameter.
3. Remove petals from the azalea flower blossoms, wash them, and wipe off the moisture. Peel off the crust of the jujubes lengthwise and mince. Remove crown daisy leaves from its stalk. Place azalea petals, minced jujubes or the crown daisy on the flat surface of dough, for frying.
4. On the oiled fry pan, put the decorated dough, and fry, at the same time pressing it with a spoon. Turn it over once and put flower petals on the top. No further turning over is necessary.
5. Apply honey over the cooked flower cake. When the azalea is not available, the cockscomb, rose, chrysanthemum, and nasturtium together with jujubes and wild astor leaves, may be used for decoration.

Suggestions

- Longer kneading makes the texture of the dough finer and softer.
- Putting decorating material on the dough, before the cake is fried, is better than putting it on after the dough is cooked. Mugwort leaves may be substituted for crown daisy leaves.

2. Cockscomb Flower Cake (*Maenturami Whajŏn*)

*W**hajŏn*** is usually made from glutinous rice flour dough, fried in the pan, on which flowers are placed in various pretty shapes. When it is done to the degree of yellowness and crunchiness, it is covered with honey and let remain for some time. People generally use the same glutinous rice flour, but its various names usually derives from the garnishing materials; in the category of flower cakes, azalea, rose, pear flower, balsam flower, cockscomb, and chrysanthemum in accordance with their blooming seasons. When no flower petals are available, sliced jujubes, mugwort leaves, or Oriental parsley are used as decorating attachments. Usually, the *whajŏn* is used as an auxiliary and decorating garnishing for major cakes.

Among the fried flower cakes, the cockscomb cake is more colorful to look at, for it is either in pink, dark crimson or white, and the entire shape of this cake looks like a cock's coronal. This gorgeous appearance helps make it taste more savory. In the light of the fact that cockscomb is used to stop diarrhea, it is natural to construe that the cockscomb pan fried cake is a natural summer food, which may help prevent a possible sign of diarrhea.

Among fried flower cakes, some have stuffing in them, which are made from round and flat dough, on which stuffing is placed in the center and then the two extreme ends are put together to make a half-moon shape on which pink, yellow and red flower petals are put for decoration. The stuffing is usually made from green pea and redbean paste.

Recipe

1. Wash and soak glutinous rice for 12 hours, drain off the water, add salt, pound and sift it to obtain fine rice flour.

❶

❷

❹

❹'

Materials and quantity

glutinous rice (powder, 10 cups)	5 cups
salt	½ Tbsp
hot water	1 cup

stuffing

cockscomb	20 blooms
jujube	10 ea
crown daisy	50 g
honey or sugar syrup	½ cup
vegetable oil	1 cup

2. Knead the rice flour with hot water, and shape a round flat dough about 5 cm in diameter.
3. Wash the cockscomb, drain off the water and remove the moisture. Peel off the crust of the jujubes lengthwise or in the shape of a flower petal. Crown daisy leaves are taken off from the stem.
4. Oil the fry pan, put the dough pieces in it, and let them cook by pressing with a spoon. Then turn them over and put cockscomb and crown daisy petals on them for decoration. No further turning is necessary.
5. Then apply honey or sugar syrup to the cooked flower cake. When the cockscomb is not available, only jujubes and crown daisies can substitute for it.

Suggestions

- Longer kneading makes the texture of the dough finer.
- Do not put too many petals on the round cake to give it a finer look, and also prevent unattractive decoration.
- Do not use an excessive amount of oil, which may change the color of the cockscomb, and also dye the color of the cockscomb flower petal to the cake body.
- When cockscomb is not available, other flower petals such as the azalea, rose, pear, peach, or chrysanthemum, may be used when they are in season.

3. Chrysanthemum Flower Cake (*Kukwhajŏn*)

According to the poem, *Nongka Wŏlryŏng Ka*, (The Songs of Month in the Farmhouse), people made yellow cake from glutinous rice and chysanthemum flower petals according to the stanza of the poem for the ninth month, September, and also in another poem, "*Tong Tong*." This means that they must have made the chrysanthemum flower cake from the earlier times and enjoyed it for a long time.

On September 9, the *chungyang* or *chungkwang* day, people went to a hill on a picnic, following their customs of the day, to enjoy the beautiful changing sundry autumn tints of the tree leaves. On such occasion, they plucked the yellow petals of chrysanthemums and made the flower cake with them.

In *Chosŏn Yori Pŏp*, the recipe of this *kukwha jŏn* is given, "Pluck the mother chrysanthemum petals and wash them in clean water. Cover them with glutinous rice flour and fry in deep oil, and then scatter cinnamon powder over it for serving."

The chrysanthemum has been appreciated from time immemorial as one of the herbals that promote the longevity of life and divine spirit. Therefore it is used both in medicine and brewery. It is also called *ŭngunja*(隱君子) or *chungyang wha*(重陽花).

On the other hand, a kind of cake known as *sŏpjŏn* is made in the Iksan region of Chullapuk-do Province, which is made from dough mixed with glutinous rice flour, liquor and water. The dough is flattened to a round shape, on which chrysanthemum leaves are placed. This is a variety of the fried ricecake *whajŏn*. This chrysanthemum *whajŏn* is loved by people for its beautiful color and fine shape, and so it is admired as the best delicacy in the late autumn.

Materials and quantity

glutinous rice (powder, 10 cups)	5 cups
salt	½ Tbsp
soju or distilled rice wine	⅓ cup
hot water	⅔ cup
chrysanthemum(small size)	30 blossoms
jujube	10 ea
chestnut	10 ea
stone mushroom	8 ea
honey or sugar syrup	½ cup
vegetable oil	1 cup

Recipe

1. Wash and soak glutinous rice for 12 hours, drain off the water, add salt, then pound and sift it to obtain fine rice flour. Add wine and hot water to it and knead the mix until it becomes soft and fine, and then make flat and round dough pieces about 5 cm in diameter (Proportion of hot water and wine is 7 to 3.).
2. Remove flower petals from the chrysanthemum blossoms, and put them onto fresh water for 10 hours, scoop and remove the remaining moisture. Peel off the crust of the jujubes lengthwise, mince it, or trim it in the shape of a flower petal. Trim the chestnuts and stone mushroom.
3. Oil the fry pan and put the dough pieces in the pan and fry. Turn it over once and place on the top decorating chrysanthemum, jujube, chestnut, on stone mushroom pieces in the shape of a flower.
4. When the *kukwhajŏn* is cooked, apply honey or sugar syrup to it. When the chrysanthemum is not available, other decoration flower petals of the azalea, yellow rose, jujube, crown daisy, etc., may be used as substitutes.

Suggestions

- The longer the kneading time, the finer and softer the dough becomes.
- Use the chrysanthemum blossom as a whole or pluck its petals, for decoration.
- Do not use too many chrysanthemum petals because they make the taste of the cake bitter.
- When an entire blossom is used, take off the green knob from it, and mix it with glutinous rice powder, knead, and fry.

4. Rose Flower Cake (*Changmi Whajŏn*)

The *whajŏn* is a fried flower cake that represents the seasonal changes very well as the flower in bloom. In the spring, the azalea flower cake is prepared; in the summer, the yellow rose flower cake; and in the fall, the chrysanthemum and the mother chrysanthemum flower cakes are enjoyed.

People use the same glutinous material all over the country, but different flower petals are placed on the rice dough, obtaining different names, accordingly. It is prepared first by kneading glutinous rice flour into dough, flat and round. After oil is put in the hot fry pan, the dough is fried in it. According to seasonal changes, azalea, rose, pear, peach, cockscomb flower petals, etc., are decorated on the fried ricecake so that we have the embellished azalea flower cake, the rose flower cake, the chrysanthemum flower cake, and the like. On the other hand, the azalea flower and leaves can be mixed to make dough with glutinous rice flour, and then fried. Honey may be applied to the cooked flower cake in order to prevent each piece from sticking together.

Other fried ricecakes, which are the same in nature with the rose flower cake, are the *chuak* and the *pukkumi*. The difference between the flower cake *whajŏn* and the *pukkumi* lies in the fact that the former doesn't have stuffing in it while the latter does, although they use the same glutinous rice flour material as a base and flower petals. To make these cakes, glutinous rice flour is kneaded with hot water into round and flat dough on which flower petals are decorated, and then fried in the pan. When either of them is deep fried, it is called *chuak*.

Materials and quantity

glutinous rice	5 cups
(or glutinous rice power, 10 cups)	
salt	½ Tbsp
hot water	1 cup
yellow rose	20 blossoms
jujube	10 ea
crown daisy	50 g
honey or sugar syrup	½ cup
vegetable oil	1 cup

Recipe

1. Wash and soak glutinous rice for 12 hours. Drain off the water, add salt, then pound and sift it to get fine rice flour.
2. Pour hot water into the rice flour, and then knead, and make round and flat pieces of dough, about 5 cm in diameter.
3. Take off the petals of a rose, wash and remove the moisture. Peel off the crust of the jujube, shred it or cut into the form of a flower petal. Pluck the leaves of the crown daisy from its stem.
4. Oil the fry pan and put in round dough pieces and cook, pressing them with a spoon. Turn them over and place yellow rose petals and crown daisy leaves on the top. No further turning over is necessary.
5. To the cooked cake, honey is applied. When yellow rose is not available, the cockscomb, azalea, chrysanthemum, jujube, or crown daisy may be used as decoration substitutes.

Suggestions

- The longer the kneading is done, the finer the dough becomes.
- It is better to place the flower petals on before frying, which makes the cake prettier to look at.
- Oil the brim of a cup or bowl which is used for shaping each round dough piece.

5. Sorghum Stuffed Cake (*Susu Pukkumi*)

The *susu pukkumi* is made from glutinous sorghum, glutinous rice, wheat, and green pea which are soaked in fresh water, and ground for kneading. As in the *chŏnpyŏng*, this kneaded dough is fried in a hot fry pan. On the flat and round fried cake are placed chestnuts, redbeans meat, and jujubes, and the center is folded so that a half-moon shaped bulging cake is produced. In this *susu pukkumi* fried cake, it is needless to say that the main ingredients are sorghum and glutinous rice.

Sorghum is a cereal that is produced in the Far Eastern countries including China and Japan, and is valued as one of the five most important grains in Korea. This cereal is analyzed as having the effect of contracting the stomach, promoting overall physical strength of a man, and lessening nausea and diarrhea. Besides being used as a staple food, sorghum is processed to make taffy, candy, cake, liquor, etc., which have been enjoyed from the earlier times in Korea.

In the olden times, besides chestnut stuffing, fresh young squash or its meat is used as stuffing. Squash is sliced, salted, squeezed, and fried, to use as stuffing, while its meat is minced and fried in the pan with various seasonings.

Pukkumi is not used as an ornamental cake, such as the topping on other cakes, but is made independently to be enjoyed. Before it is put on the plate and set on the table for serving, it is covered with honey or sugar to prevent its pieces from sticking together.

Susu pukkumi is naturally, traditionally, and widely made in Whanghae-do Province of central Korea, where sorghum is abundantly grown and harvested. The outward look of this cake is not so gorgeous and its color is rather dim, but its shape is distinctive so that it seems to radiate the pleasant flavor of one's hometown in a sense.

Recipe

1. Wash sorghum and soak it in fresh water over night to get rid of astringents. Add salt and pound it.

Materials and quantity

- glutinous sorghum .... 5 cups (or its powder, 10 cups)
- salt .... 1 Tbsp

redbean stuffing

- redbean(roughly ground) . 2 cups
- salt .... 1 tsp
- sugar or honey .... 4 tsp
- cinnamon powder .... 1 tsp

jujube .... 10 ea
pinenut .... 2 Tbsps
vegetable oil ...... a small quantity
sugar .... 2 Tbsps

2. Soak redbeans in water, and remove their outer crusts and other improper elements, such as sand and broken pieces of redbean twigs. Steam them sufficiently and sift them through a rough grid sieve. Add sugar, salt, and cinnamon powder to them, mix them well and make a small oval ball stuffing.
3. Knead the sorghum dough, and detach a piece of it. Then make a ball, and flatten, 6 cm in diameter.
4. Oil the fry pan, and put the round dough in the fry pan. Then put the stuffing in the center of the flattened dough, put the two extreme ends together, and press the remaining round edge thoroughly in the shape of a half-moon. Decorate it with jujubes and pinenuts. While the cake is still hot, scatter sugar over it for serving.

Suggestion

- Rub glutinous sorghum and wash away red juice oozing out from it, soak it in fresh water to remove astringent element, drain off the water and pound it to make its flour.
- Knead the sorghum dough sufficiently, thereby it will not get cracked when frying. Fry it over light heat so that it will not inflate excessively.
- The stuffing on the dough should be plump so that the final cake form will appear pretty. Decorative flowers can be realized in various forms.

6. Fried Cake (*Chuak*)

C huak is also one of the fried cakes. In the palace it was called *choak*, while among the common folks, it was known as *chuak*. This differs from the flower cake *whajŏn*, in that it is a deep fried cake. To the dough made from pure glutinous rice flour, are put pounded jujubes, sesame seeds, citron, etc., as filling and it is made into a half moon shaped bulging cake, like the *songp'yŏn*, and then deep fried.

In the *Sumun Sasŏl* published in 1740, this cake is recorded for the first time, where it is listed as the *choyakjŏn*, and in the *Kyuhap Chongsŏ* of 1815, there appeared the chestnut and jujube *chuak* with the following recipe; "The chestnut *chuak* is made with dried chestnut pieces, first mixed with honey, and then to this added as stuffing are pinenuts, cinnamon, and dried ginger particles. It is made like a half-moon shaped *songp'yŏn*. The book also says, "To the outer surface of the crust, honey is applied and then pinenut particles are dredged over its honeyed surface. When glutinous rice flour is kneaded with fresh water, it tastes soft and palatable, but too chewy when kneaded with warm or hot water. Even in frying, only a few pieces must be put into simmering oil at a time and scooped out of the oil soon so as to prevent them from sticking to each other." From this, we can assume that its size must have been smaller than that of the one we enjoy in present days.

In some ancient records, it is named the *choakjŏn*, or the *chogakpyŏng*. In the *Sumun Sasŏl*, it says, "The *choakjŏn* is made from rice flour kneaded with sweetened water, and sugar is used as a stuffing. It is deep fried." On the other hand in the *Imwŏn Sipyukji*, the *chokagpyŏng* was highly valued.

In other documents, the ingredients of this cake are listed as glutinous rice, redbean, black beans, laver seaweed, sesame seed, chestnut, pinenut, ginkgo, mugwort, *sonko*, cinnamon, gardenia seed, honey, sesame oil, etc.

Materials and quantity

- glutinous rice .... 2 cups (powder, 4 cups)
- salt .... 1 tsp
- hot water .... a little

- gardenia seed .... 2 cracked pieces
- mugwort .... 20 g
- *omija*(five-tastes) seed .... 1 Tbsp
- coloring additive .... a little quantity

stuffing

- seared sesame .... ⅓ cup
- honey .... 1 Tbsp
- salt .... ½ tsp
- cinnamon powder .... ⅛ tsp

- jujube .... 8 ea
- honey .... 1 Tbsp
- cinnamon powder .... ⅛ tsp

- vegetable oil .... 3 Tbsps
- honey .... ½ cup
- cinnamon powder .... 1 tsp
- minced pinenut .. a little amount

Recipe

1. Make glutinous rice flour and sift it to obtain fineness.
2. Divide the rice powder into four parts, add to the divided powder such coloring elements as the jujube, chestnut, angelica, ginkgo, stone mushroom, and gardenia, to make respective *juak*, such as jujube *juak* in red, stone mushroom *juak* in black, etc.
3. For sesame stuffing, sear sesame in the fry pan, add honey and salt, and mix them up. For jujube stuffing, peel off the crust of the jujube lengthwise, and mince it, and add honey and cinnamon powder, mixing them together.
4. Knead the glutinous rice powder, and take off a small amount from the dough, and make it into a ball, then press to make a flat round patch. Put one kind of stuffing in the center of the flattened dough and put the two extreme ends of dough together, pressing them hard; the remaining edges are also pressed tightly.
5. Fry the rugby ball shaped *juak* in 150℃ oil, put away in honey with cinnamon powder, and spray minced pinenuts on it when serving.

7. Fried *Tŏtŏk* Cake (*Sŏpsan Sampyŏng*)

This fried cake first appeared in the *Ŭmsik Timipang*, written in the Korean Hangul alphabet in 1670, in the earlier years of King Sukjŏng's reign, by CHANG Ji-young, wife of YI Shi-young living in Yŏngyang-kun, Kyŏngsanpuk-do Province. Its main ingredients are *tŏtŏk*, glutinous rice flour, and honey. Its recipe says, "Peel off the skin of fresh *tŏtŏk*, pound its meat, which is then soaked in fresh water to get rid of its bitter flavor, and pound it again softly, cover it with coarse hemp cloth to squeeze out the water. Then cover it with glutinous rice flour for deep frying. The fried pieces are covered with honey." This is served as a side dish auxiliary to drinking these days.

The term 'fried *tŏtŏk* cake' was variously called in the earlier times, such as *sŏpsan sanpyŏng*, *sampyŏng*, *sasampyŏng*, *kaksaek sansam*, etc., whose ingredients are, besides *tŏtŏk*, glutinous rice flour and honey, gardenia seed, oil, red coloring agent, etc.

The root of *tŏtŏk* (*codonopsis lanceolata*) is rich in saponin contents, which is removed by immersing it in warm water so that stickiness caused by saponin will be lessened. *Tŏtŏk* is well known for its stimulating effects on the stomach, and for its promoting effect of robustness on the kidney, the lungs, and the spleen, and accordingly, used as medicine for these effects.

In the autumn when *tŏtŏk* is in season, it becomes thick and white. Its erect roots are valued highly for their richness in nutrients and medicinal contents. It is used variously for its particular taste and flavor in ordinary meal dishes, and it is preserved in red pepper paste as a delicacy.

Materials and quantity

tŏtŏk	2 ½ Kg
salt	3 tsps
glutinous rice powder	9 cups
sugar or honey	1 cup
vegetable oil	a small amount

Recipe

1. Peel off the crust of tŏtŏk. A long one is cut into two pieces, lengthwise, and pounded with a wooden pounder to make them flat and expanded.
2. Soak them in water and allow the bitter taste element to leave, drain off the water, wipe off any remaining moisture, and then add salt to them.
3. Apply sesame oil to the lightly salted *tŏtŏk* thoroughly, and press it with the hands, put into hot oil at 160℃ and let it fry until it becomes yellowish. Scoop it from the oil and spray sugar or apply honey. It makes a good side dish for liquor drinking. Vinegar with soybean sauce is used along with it.

Suggestions

- Thick and straight *tŏtŏk* is valued. Cut it into two lengthwise and be careful not to have a part torn off. Its pounding is done on the chopping board. Soak it in fresh water to get rid of its bitter taste before frying.
- When peeling off its crust, first broil it lightly and scratch off its crust. This is an easier way of peeling its crust without having its sticky element sticking to one's hands.

1. Multi-Colored Rice Balls (*Kaksaek Kyŏngdan*) **Samnŭn Ttŏk**

These multi-colored rice balls are made from glutinous rice flour, kneaded into a ball, dipped in simmering hot water, and then dredging of sundry colored garnishing is done, one color for a ball. In a documented recipe of the Chosŏn Dynasty, *kyŏngdan* is made from glutinous rice flour, which is kneaded and sliced to the size and shape of the *chuak* or the *yakkwa*, or a hole is made in the center, and then the dough is dipped in simmering water for a while, then scooped to have garnishing dredged around it. It is also called *chapkwa.*

The glutinous rice *kyŏngdan* was first recorded as *kyŏndang pyŏng*, in the *Yorok* published in 1680, which gives the same recipe as illustrated in the above. In a later book, *Chŭngbo Sanrim Kyŏngjae* of 1766, the 4th year of King Yŏngjo's reign, it was listed simply as *kyŏngdan*, whose recipe is a little different. The book relates, "Buckwheat flour is kneaded a bit watery with honeyed water, putting the dough into earthenware, cover its mouth tightly, and put into a husk fire, and let remain until the wateriness of the dough is evaporated. It tastes very sweet. Or take out the cake using a spoon and mold it in the shape of the *song-p'yŏn* and sprinkle sesame over it to augment its flavor and taste." In the *Imwŏn Simyukji*, a rice ball cake of the same name which uses ginger juice, is mentioned. In the *Chosŏn Yori Pŏp* of 1938, a further difference in major ingredients is observed in that sorghum flour, honey stuffing, and roasted bean powder are used, and a different cooking procedure is also presented.

For the *kyŏngdan*, roasted bean powder, mashed redbean particles and roasted sesame are used, and from whose materials, *kyŏndang* is given its modifying and differentiating names, such as *k'ong kyŏngdang* with bean powder, *pam kyŏngdan* with chestnuts, *kep'i kyŏngdan* with cinnamon, *chat kyŏngdan* with pinenuts, etc. The cereal ball cake made from glutinous sorghum is commonly called sorghum redbean cake, *susup'at ttŏk.*

Materials and quantity

glutinous rice .... 5 cups
(its flour, 10 cups)
salt .... 1 Tbsp

yellow bean powder .... ½ cup
green bean powder .... ½ cup
black sesame .... ½ cup
redbean with its crust removed .... ½ cup
redbean .... ½ cup
salt .... 1 Tbsp
sugar .... ½ cup

Suggestions

- To make *kyŏndan*, knead the glutinous rice flour with hot water. When boiling, stir the rice balls often so that they do not get stuck to one another or go down to the bottom of the pan. When the rice balls are boiled sufficiently, they emerge to the surface. Scoop them out, chill them in cold water, and remove the moisture.
- Redbeans, jujubes, green beans, black sesame, etc., can be used as dredging.

Recipe

1. Wash and soak glutinous rice for 12 hours, drain off the water, add salt, then pound and sift it to obtain finer rice flour.
2. Knead the glutinous rice powder with hot water, and make small balls about 2 cm in diameter. Put the ball shaped dough in the boiling water until it is poached, and then put it in cold water until it gets cool.
3. Sear black sesame, pound it in a mortar and sift it. Soak both redbeans and beans with their crusts removed, separately, and rub them to get rid of their crusts and steam or boil them. When boiling, parboil them, remove the water and input fresh water again and cook until they become soft. Then drain off the hot water and leave them over low heat for maturing. Add salt to them and knead with a flat wooden scoop, then sift them to make dredging. Put sugar into the redbean dredging, but not to the beans with no crust.
4. Divide balls into five parts to add five different colored dredgings to them.

2. Glutinous Millet Cake (*Omegi Ttŏk*)

This millet cake is made from Italian millet, which is made into a powder, kneaded into round dough, and dredged with yellowish bean powder. In Cheju-do Island, these days, it is made like a doughnut with a hallow hole in the center, and dipped in sweet syrup before serving. Glutinous millet is in two colors; one in yellow, the other, black. The latter is used for cakes.

Millet can be preserved easily and longer. According to the *Kerim Yusa*(鷄林類事), Kokuryŏ had a bountiful millet harvest among the five important staple cereals, which reflects naturally that millet is a well-breeding cereal in the northern area. Even today, quality millet is abundantly produced in North Korea. Millet is cooked for meal with rice and is also used variously in cakes. In olden times, when a rich man had white ricecake *hŭin ttŏk*, or the glutinous ricecake *injŏlmi*, pounded on a flat board or in a mortar, the pounding sound echoed through the village, whereby villagers were attracted to come to the scene. Then the millet was washed, steamed in a steaming vessel, *siru*, and made into cakes. The onlooking villagers were treated with pieces of the millet cake, each piece to one individual so that they could get rid of their hungry feeling while watching. From this we can construe that millet was the very cereal for the humble people.

The main ingredients of millet are protein and fat, whose absorption is higher than that of barley. It contains a lot of vitamins B_1 and B_2, and promotes the function of the kidneys. Its dried sprouts are called *chokŭmkil* and used in herbal medicine for their effectiveness in curing indigestion and stomach upset, and in promoting the appetite.

Materials and quantity

glutinous Italian millet (powder, 10 cups)		5 cups
salt		1 Tbsp

stuffing

bean powder	3 cups
salt	½ tsp
sugar	3 Tbsp
redbean	1 cup
salt	1 tsp
sugar	2 Tbsp

Suggestions

- When you make a ring of millet dough, first make it a rather thick ball. Make a space in the center, pressing with a thumb.
- Remove as much moisture as possible when the millet dough is chilled in fresh water, after being boiled in the boiling water. This helps dredging to adhere to the ring surface evenly.
- This *omeki ttŏk* is tasty while it is still warm; so serve it before it gets cool.

Recipe

1. Wash glutinous Italian millet, removing foreign elements, and soak it in fresh water for 5~6 hours, drain off the water, add salt to it, then pound and sift it to get fine millet powder.
2. Wash the beans, drain off the water, remove the moisture, sear and grind them in a rotating grinder, then sift them and add salt and sugar to them for seasoning.
3. Boil redbeans sufficiently in water, drain off the water, add salt, sift them through a rough net sieve, and add sugar.
4. Knead the millet flour with hot water, make a doughnut shape ring, about 5 cm in diameter. Poach the ring in boiling water, and chill it in fresh water. When the water is drained off sufficiently, cover the ball with either bean powder or redbean dredging for serving.

3. Thick Ball Cake (*Tut'ŏp Tanja*)

T*ut'ŏp tanja* belongs to the ball cake category, *tanjapyŏng*(單子餅類), like *songp'yŏn*, *kyŏngdan*, etc., which are prepared by boiling, simmering, or steaming. *Songp'yŏn* is made from regular rice, whereas the dough of *tanja* and *kyŏngdan*, glutinous rice, by is dipping in boiling water, and then dredging.

Tut'ŏp tanja is made through the following procedure: glutinous rice flour is kneaded with hot water into a round flat dough, in the center of which are placed chestnuts, walnuts, pine-nuts, jujubes, or sweetened citron as a filling. Its opening is closed with the fingers; the round dough is then put into boiling water and let remain until it surfaces. It is scooped out of the boiling water for dredging with soft mashed redbean particles. When its kneaded dough is covered with a wet cloth and allowed to set for a while for thorough dampening, it becomes very chewy.

The size of the *tut'ŏp tanja* is usually larger than that of the *kyŏndan*, for which the *tut'ŏp tanja* gives a better outward appearance. Its dough is made by rolling it so that a better looking shape is formed. Then, two or three pieces of the cake are put into simmering water at a time and scooped out of it when they emerge onto the surface of the hot water. They are then put into cold running water, after which they are put onto the dredging powder and swayed so that dredging will be done very beautifully. This cake is very soft to eat, and produces a special flavor and taste by having stuffed dried fruits and citron mingle harmoniously with the redbean powder of dredg-ing, whereby concocting a special delicacy.

Recipe

1. Wash glutinous rice, removing foreign elements, soak it in fresh water for 12 hours, drain off the water, add salt, then pound and sift it to obtain a fine glutinous rice flour. When the powder is lacking in moisture, spray water and rub it with hands, and sift it again. Knead it with hot sugar syrup.
2. Grind the redbeans and put them into water, drain upper water and put their sediment into a fry pan and sear them. Boil sugar syrup, let it cool, mix it with the redbean sediment, and sift the mix.
3. Peel off the outer crust of the chestnuts and also their inner covering, and slice to a 0.5 cm thickness, and put the sliced pieces into sugar syrup, allowing the sugar to penetrate into the chestnut pieces, and hard boil them. Crack the walnuts and soak their meat in hot water, removing the inner covering off the meat. Slice it as thick as the chestnut piece and trim it. Remove the core seed from the jujube and knead it with the citron in syrup, add citron syrup, and mix well to make stuffing.
4. Make balls out of kneaded dough of glutinous rice, make a space in the ball's center with the thumb, put stuffing into the center space, and cover the space tightly by pressing the ball with the hands so that the dough ball is made into one 5 cm in diameter.
5. Put the dough pieces into boiling water, scoop them out, put them into cool fresh water, and scoop one by one, then remove the moisture and put the redbean dredging around the flat ball cake.

Materials and quantity

glutinous rice	2 cups
(powder, 4 cups)	
salt	1 tsp
sugar syrup	1 and ⅔ cups
(water 1 cup, sugar ⅔ cup)	

stuffing

redbean powder	½ cup
chestnut	4 ea
walnut	3 ea
pinenut	½ Tbsp
jujube	4 ea
citron syrup	2 Tbsp

2. The Origins and Development of Korea Cookies

The Korean traditional sweets are called *kwajŏn ryu*(果釘類) and differentiated from the cakes *kwaja*(菓子) originated from foreign countries. The Korean traditional sweets consist of *yumilkwa* or *suksilkwa*(oil-honey pastry, 油密果), *tasik* (pattern-pressed pastry, 茶食), *chŏngkwa*(candied fruits, 正果, 煎果), *kwapyŏn*(fruit pastry, 果餅), *yŏt kangjŏng*(taffy cookie), etc.

These cookies are made from cereals and honey, and set up on the table or altar of votive offering to one's forefathers. When fruits were available, they were used as sacrifices, but when they were not, these processed cookies with branches of fruit trees stuck into them, were presented instead. But these days, both fruits and its substitutes are used at the same time regardless of season. According as farming developed to produce more cereals, and the further promulgation of Buddhism which teaches its followers not to eat animal meat, these types of cookies flourished enormously as indispensable substitute foods on the occasions of worshiping forefathers, and at weddings and banquets, especially in the ages of the ancient Kokuryŏ and Shilla kingdoms.

Koreans may have used oil and honey to make cookies earlier, but people started using these materials widely and sufficiently in sweets after the Three Kingdoms had been unified into one. The custom of preparing sweets ancillary to tea drinking, thrived during those periods. It was because Buddhism flourished especially during the unified Shilla Kingdom period. In the later years of the unified Kingdom, many tea related ceremonies were organized and conducted, such as a ceremony of tea and sweets, a tea ceremony, and a tea arbor ceremony, through which sweets were further developed and flourished.

In the ensuing Koryŏ Dynasty, Buddhism was adopted as the nation saving religion, and killing animals was prohibited and the consumption of its meat was also withheld so that people were more inclined to develop and consume sweets along with the habit of drinking tea. Among the sweets, the oil-and-honey cookie was especially developed so that it became a must to be stacked high up on the altar at temple ceremonies, large or small, such as the lantern ceremony, the *palkwanhŭi* ceremony(八關會), in which indigenous deities were worshipped and put to repose, and other such events.

The Korean oil-and-honey pastry *yumilkwa* spread to foreign countries; in Mongolia, where this cookie was known as *Koryŏ pyŏng*, or *yakkwa*(藥果) and enjoyed as a delicacy.

In the later period of the Chosŏn Dynasty, the sweets were included without fail among the dishes to be set up on the king's dining table. They were also representative items to be set up on the dining table of a man celebrating some happy event. These sweets were enjoyed to a great extent not only as items of formal occasions, but also as common delicacies, especially among royal and aristocratic families.

Meanwhile the taffy cereal cookie, *kanjŏng*, was more popular than any other cookies among the common folks, which was usually prepared for the new year's day, which is one of the most important holidays in Korea. For fun, some people preferred to compete with each other when they made the cookies to see who had the most excellent skill of making the largest one.

Along with the oil-and-honey cookie, deep fried cakes, pattern-pressed pastry, and candied fruits were widely and commonly enjoyed. A total of 255 varieties of sweets were recorded during this dynasty, which breaks down to 37 oil-and-honey cookies, 68 fried cookies, 28 pattern-pressed pastry, 51 candied fruits, 11 candied sour fruits, 6 taffy cereal cookies and 53 sweet candies. From this large quantity of sweets, one can say that Koreas must have been very keen connoisseurs of sweets.

The oil-and-honey pastry is made from kneaded cereal powder, which is then fried in oil; the pattern-pressed pastry is made from cereal powder mixed with honey and then pressed in the mold; the fruit cookie is made from fresh fruits or their roots which are sweetened with caramel or honey, removing its moisture; the candied sour fruit is made from fruits, which are completely dissolved in boiling water, filtered, and then made like gelatine when the solution gets cold; the fruit candy is made from fruits mixed with other materials and boiled; and the taffy cookie is made from nuts which are mixed with cereals and warm caramel *choch'ŏng*. All these are common heritages that the present-day Koreans are proud of.

1. Fried Cookie (*Yakkwa*, 藥果)

Yumilkwa

One of the cookies, not to mention the oil-and-honey cookies which have been enjoyed as quality sweets, is the *yakkwa.* It is one of the most representative cookies that are prepared for the new year's day to worship one's forefathers and for celebrating festivities including weddings. The oil-and-honey cookies were regarded as luxurious foods, and during the remaining years of the Koryŏ Dynasty a large quantity of cereals was consumed to make these delicacies by the aristocratic families and Buddhist temples, whereby the price of cereals went up to influence common people's living costs so much that King Kongmin prohibited people from making these sweets in his second year of reign, 1353.

During the Chosŏn Dynasty period, the *yakkwa* was regarded as the most favorite and representative pastry and relished among the royal families and upper aristocratic homes. It was also an indispensable food item served on the altar of worshipping forefathers, and on the dining table for guests, on new year's day, and treated as an essential food of rites to be set up for celebrating festivities. The *yak* in *yakkwa* means medicine, but its original meaning derives from honey, which is nicknamed *yak.* From this word *yak* with its meaning 'honey', people call honey liquor *yakju*; honeyed rice, *yakpap*; and honey and fruit, *yakkwa.*

The form of *yakkwa* went through several steps, such as, that of jujubes, chestnuts, pears, persimmons, birds, or animals, and eventually took a round form during the Chosŏn Dynasty. Later it took a square form to make it easier to set up on the altar or table, but it was transformed into a round form again, and finally came to be pressed on the *yakkwa* pattern board.

Materials and quanlity

- wheat flour(weakly cohesive) ··· 30 Tbsp (2 cups, 220 g)
- sesame oil ··· 3 Tbsp
- honey ··· 3 Tbsp
- rice wine ··· 2 Tbsp
- salt ··· ¼ tsp
- ginger syrup ··· 2 Tbsp
- grey black pepper ··· ¼ tsp

honey mix

- transparent honey ··· 1 cup
- cinnamon powder ··· ½ tsp

shredded pinenut ··· 3 Tbsp

vegetable oil for frying ··· 2 cups

Recipe

1. Sift wheat flour, add sesame oil to it little by little, rubbing the mixture at the same time with the hands, and sift again.
2. Mix together honey, wine, salt, ginger juice, and grey black pepper, and knead the mixture with the flour as in the case of making a large dough mass.
3. Coat the *yakkwa* pattern frame with oil, and detach about 50 g of dough, place it in the pattern frame, and press hard with fingers. Take the patterned dough out of the press, and make 6~7 holes to the rear side for the oil to penetrate into the cake easily.
4. Slowly fry the patterned dough in vegetable oil at 140℃~150℃. Fry one side for 4 minutes and turn it over and fry the other side for 3 minutes.
5. When the dough is changed into a brown color, scoop it out of the oil, let the oil drip from it, and allow its temperature to go down. Put the cake in the honey mix, leave it there for 12 hours, then take it out and spray shredded pinenut over it for serving.

2. Plum Sparrow Cookie (*Maejakkwa*, 梅雀果)

This *maejakkwa* gained its name from its shape, which was interpreted as a sparrow resting on a plum tree. It has various other denominations, such as, the *maejitkwa*, the *maejapkwa*, the *maeyŏpkwa* and the *t'arae*, although they are made in the same way and taste alike. Korean traditional cookies were called, on the other hand, imitation or substitution cookies, because they took the place of real fruits when they were needed but not available, on the occasions of setting up the altar for worshipping forefathers.

As mentioned elsewhere, Korean cookies were made to consume with tea, whereby enormous development ensued in the Kokuryŏ and Shilla Kingdoms. These favorable changes were possible because farming techniques were developed, which resulted in the more bountiful production of cereals, and at the same time, in line with the wider promulgation of Buddhism, the consumption of animal meat was forbidden, which naturally motivated people to find their way into cereal cookies.

The *maejakkwa* is an oil-and-honey cookie made with dough of wheat flour mixed with salt and ginger. The dough is flattened and carved with a knife in the shape of a river. Then it is turned over and put into simmering oil for frying, scooped out and honey added. It tastes savory and sweet with the flavor of ginger and cinnamon, and is also crispy. It is easy to make this cookie pretty at any time, so it is often found on the tea table for a guest. It is customary to stack up a larger *yakkwa* on an elaborate and ceremonial table, whereas it is common to serve the pattern-pressed pastry, the *yakkwa*, or plum-sparrow cookies for a meal or on a tea table.

Materials and quantity

wheat flour	1 cup
salt	⅛ tsp
ginger	20 g
honey mix	
honey	1 cup
cinnamon powder	½ tsp
minced pinenut	1 Tbsp
fry-powder	3 cups

Recipe

1. Mix wheat flour with salt and sift it through a fine grid sieve, add ginger juice and water to it, kneading until the dough becomes soft.
2. Flatten the dough to about 0. 3 cm thickness, and cut it into 5 cm×2. 5 cm pieces. Draw three lines like water flowing, i.e., 川, and fold the two side edges at one end, and then push the folded part to be reversed through the center line.
3. Put each piece into clean oil at 140℃~150℃ one by one in such a way that they do not get deformed. When the dough turns yellow, remove it from the oil and let the remaining oil drip off. Put it into honey mix and store in a container. Before serving, spray minced pinenuts over it.

Suggestions

- Dough should be flattened very thin like paper.
- Use clean oil to get crispy plum sparrow cookies, *maejakkwa*.
- Dough may be made into noodles, and woven by twisting, cut into 6 cm long pieces, and fried.
- Instead of honey, sugar syrup can be made with 1 cup of sugar and 1 cup of water. Add cinnamon powder to sugar syrup, and coat the cake ten minutes before serving. Care must be given not to stir the sugar syrup while it is being made, for such action helps the syrup return to the original state of sugar.

3. Honeyed Chestnut and Honeyed Jujube
(*Pamch'o* and *Taech'uch'o*)

The word *ch'o* means nuts whose meat is boiled down in honeyed liquid. Among many honeyed nuts, the honeyed chestnut and jujube are the most popular.

Pamch'o is made by boiling down chestnuts in honeyed liquid. An old saying goes like this, "If you eat three chestnuts a day, you won't need any stimulants for physical vitality." True to this proverb, the chestnut has very rich nutrients. The good quality chestnut is heavy and has a lustrous crust. To make the *pamch'o*, one has to pick up large and fresh chestnuts, peel off the hard crusts and inner endodermis and carve them into a beautiful shape. Dried chestnuts in yellow may be used instead, by soaking and boiling them in water.

The jujube *taech'ucho* is made in the same way as the honeyed chestnut. Jujubes are used widely in herbal medicine since they have the effect of strengthening the liver's function and overall physiological functions. On the other hand, jujubes are regarded, according to Korean folklore, to symbolize the prosperity of posterity, so they are thrown over the spread skirt of a bride, praying that the bride will give birth to a large number of children for the family's prosperity. In folk medicine, the jujube is used to treat mental depression; the bitter element of the jujubes is effective in soothing and lessening mental strain, and also effective in coping with hysteria and various menopause symptoms.

Materials and quantity

Honeyed chestnut, *pamch'o*

chestnut .... 20 ea
salt .... 1 tsp
honey, sugar syrup, or glucose .... ⅔ cup

Honeyed jujube, *taech'uch'o*

jujube .... 25 ea
pinenut .... 2 Tbsp
honey, sugar, or glucose .... ⅔ cup
cinnamon powder .... ¼ tsp
minced pinenut .... 1 Tbsp

Recipe

Honeyed chestnut, *pamch'o*

1. Peel off the crust of the chestnut and trim it in good shape, immersing it in hot salted water.
2. Put chestnuts and honey into a kettle and put the mix over high heat at first, then over low heat later to braise.
3. Remove any foam or foreign material on the surface. When the honeyed syrup is almost gone, add cinnamon powder to it to make it lustrous.
4. Put it in the container and spray minced pinenuts over it to give a pleasant look.

Honeyed jujube, *taech'uch'o*

1. Wipe a jujube with a wet cloth, peel off its crust lengthwise, and apply honey to the inside of the crust. Put three pinenuts on the inside of the jujube crust and roll it up and press hard for them to stay together.
2. Mix honey, cinnamon powder, and jujubes together, boil the mix over high heat, and then low heat to get it braised slowly. Remove often any foam being formed, and spray honeyed syrup over it. After braising, put pinenuts to both ends of the rolled jujube crust. A honeyed jujube may be served together with honeyed chestnuts with minced pinenuts scattered over them.

4. Taffy Cookie (*Yŏtkangjŏng*)

The taffy cookie, *yŏtkangjŏng*, is made from cereals or nuts kneaded in caramel or taffy liquid. The sticky mixture is put into a tray for flattening with a roller and sliced into pieces when it is still warm and soft. Here, taffy liquid works as glue to cause grains to stick to each other, and therefore a lesser amount is used for taffy cookies than when taffy candy is made. However, one caveat is that a balanced combination of taffy, sugar and water makes it right. Taffy alone makes a taffy cookie too soft, and sugar alone, too crispy, and so their balance in quantity is important. The final outcome is usually square pieces, but rolled round pieces with a pattern are also made. The taffy cookie of white sesame is often decorated beautifully with pine-nut or jujube garnishing.

The taffy cookies are classified depending on the major ingredients, such as, black sesame, green perilla, white sesame and green bean, roasted black bean, peanut, walnut, and pine-nut taffy cookies.

In the olden days, people prepared taffy cookies around the new year's day or in the spring and stored them in a cool jar, and used them in the new year's day celebration and offered them to guests. Since the taffy cookies are rich in protein, fat and minerals, they are good for snacks and can be a delicious dessert along with tea.

Materials and quantity

pinenut	1 cup
peanut	1 cup
white sesame	1 cup
perilla	1 cup
black sesame	1 cup
sugar	2 cups
glucose syrup	1 cup
water	1 cup
dredging	
jujube	10 ea
pinenut	2 Tbsp
walnut	10 ea
honey	1 Tbsp
vegetable oil	2 Tbsp

Recipe

1. Trim pinenuts and peanuts, and cut a peanut into four pieces.
2. Rub white sesame, get rid of its crust, and sear it lightly. Remove foreign elements from black sesame and perilla, and sear them lightly.
3. Put sugar and water into a pan and boil the mix until its quantity lessens to a half. Scoop it and let it fall. If the mixed syrup falls as a mass, then put the syrup onto the peanut, white sesame, etc., and mix them well with a flat wooden scoop so that they eventually become sticky.
4. Oil a flat tray, put a taffy cookie onto it, and flatten it immediately with a roller to about 5 cm thick. Apply sugar syrup over the taffy cookie and scatter minced jujubes, press the mixture with a roller, and cut it into square pieces before it gets congealed. Pinenuts and walnuts are coated over the cookie pieces as dredging.
5. Perilla and black sesame can be stacked together, rolled, and sliced, and then a beautiful pattern of *t'aeguk* will appear.

5. Pattern-Pressed Pastry (*Tasik*)

T*asik* is made from roasted cereal powder or pine blossom pollen kneaded with honey, and pressed into various flower designs or Chinese character patterns. According to the *Samkuk Yusa*, "It originated from the custom of making it with tea leaves, and offering it as a sacrifice to worship forefathers, in the Three Kingdom Period." There are a wide variety in its major ingredients. In the *Kyuhap Ch'ongsŏ*, there are listed dried chestnuts, longan herb(龍顔肉), black sesame, starch *tasik*, etc., together with their cookery. Sugar and honey were used as the congealing agents. On the other hand, in 'The Korean Cookery', in comparison with the common practice of using cereals as major ingredients, several kinds of fish are also described in making this kind of pastry, such as fried perch, dried perch, and flatfish. Equally particular is the fact that sesame oil, water and black pepper are listed as congealing agents.

The sweet taste of *tasik* mingles with its major ingredients, which generates particular tastes of its own depending on its major ingredients. Naturally, *tasik* has picked up several names depending on its major ingredients, such as *songwha tasik* with pine blossoms, *sŭngkŏmch'o tasik* with angelica and pine blossom, *nokmal tasik* with starch, *pam tasik* with dried chestnut powder, *ssal tasik* with glutinous rice flour, *saengkang tasik* with ginger, etc.

Tasik is an indispensable item to be prepared for weddings, sixtieth birthday celebrations, and forefather worshipping rites.

Materials and quantity

black sesame	2 cups
honey	½~⅔ cup
choch'ŏng syrup	2 Tbsp
seared glutinous rice powder	3 cups
salt ⅛ Tbsp, honey	5 Tbsp
choch'ŏng syrup	7 Tbsp
pine flower powder	3 cups
honey	1 Tbsp
choch'ŏng syrup	5 Tbsp
bean powder	2 cups
honey	⅓ cup
choch'ŏng syrup	2 Tbsp
green pea starch powder	1 cup
omija juice(*omija* seed, ¼ cup+water, ½ cup)	2 tsps
honey	1 Tbsp
choch'ŏng syrup	2 Tbsp
angelica powder	2 Tbsp
pine flower powder, or green bean powder	2 cups
honey	2 tsps
choch'ŏng syrup	4 Tbsp
sesame oil	a small quantity

Recipe

1. Sear black sesame lightly, pound and sift it. Sear also glutinous rice and beans lightly, pound and sift them. Prepare pine flower (blossom) powder and starch powder.
2. Put black sesame in the steamer and steam lightly, then put it into the mortar and pound until its oil oozes out. Then add honey, and *choch'ŏng* syrup to it and mix them together. Oil it and put the mix into pattern frame and push hard with fingers, and remove the patterned *tasik*.
3. Knead the seared glutinous rice powder, pine flower powder, and bean powder, separately, with honey and *choch'ŏng* syrup, and mould them into the *tasik* pattern following the same procedure as black sesame pattern-pressed pastry.
4. Mix together green pea starch, five-taste seed juice, honey and *choch'ŏng* syrup, and knead the mix and put it into the pattern-press, press it hard, and then take out the *tasik* piece.
5. Mix the angelica powder and the pine flower powder, and to the mix honey and *choch'ŏng* syrup. Knead the mix and put it into the mould pattern and press hard.

6. Taffy Pop Cookie (*Kangjŏng*)

This type of taffy cookie is produced in the same way as *sanja*; they differ only in shape, the round one is *kangjŏng*, and the flat square piece, *sanja*. Their dough is made from glutinous rice flour, which is cut into round or flat square pieces. They are then let stay for a while for their moisture to dry, fried, and then covered with honey and dredging. The dough can be made into small pieces of redbean size, which are fried and congealed with taffy liquid, and then cut into neat pieces with a knife. It is called *pingsakwa*(氷似果), the ice-like cookie.

An earlier written recipe found in the *Kyukonsiŭi Pang* is observed even today so far as its basics are concerned. It says, "Knead glutinous rice flour with fermenting liquor and bean juice, and steam it, then knead again until small air pockets are formed in it, let it dry, and fry it in boiling oil for the dough to pop up. Apply honey on the fried pieces and dredge them with white sesame, fried and popped colored rice, angelica powder, or the like."

The taffy pop cookie also has several names depending on its dredging materials, such as the *kkae kangjŏng* with sesame; the *chat kangjŏng* with pinenuts; the *kh'ŏng kangjŏng* with beans; the *songwha kangjŏng* with pine pollen; the *tangkwi kangjŏng* with angelica root powder, etc. Meanwhile, *sanja* has its various denominations depending on the color of rice used as its dredging: the *paek sanja* in white; the *hong sanja* in red; and the *maewha sanja* in yellow.

The taffy pop cookies are served on elaborate meal tables, and also on the altar for worshiping forefathers. It is one of the representative foods that must be prepared for the new year's day, along with ricecake and soup and ginger-cinnamon *sujŏngkwa*. The charm of this kind of oiled honey cake is its crispiness when chewed and ensuing watering when it begins melting in the mouth.

Materials and quantity

glutinous rice .... 5 cups
rice wine .... 3 Tbsp
sugar .... 3 Tbsp
vegetable oil .... a little quantity

Bean syrup

- soaked white bean .... ½ cup
- water .... ½ cup

honey mix

- sugar syrup .... 1 cup
- honey .... 5 Tbsp

dredging

white sesame, black sesame, popped rice, bean powder, angelica powder

Recipe

1. Wash glutinous rice, and soak it in water for one or two weeks. If scum develops, wash the glutinous rice several times, and sift it.
2. Mix well-sifted glutinous rice, wine, sugar, and bean syrup, little by little, with a flat wooden scoop, and knead it to the extent that dough is formed.
3. Place a wet hemp cloth on the bottom of the steamer, put in the dough mass, and steam sufficiently. Put the steamed dough into a large vessel and knead with a wooden bar to the extent that foam is formed. Stretch the dough by pulling it up many times so that air pockets are formed in the dough.
4. Spray the dry rice powder or the starch powder on a flat wooden board, bring the dough over it and flatten the dough to the thickness of 0.5 cm with a wooden roller, and let it chill. Then cut it into pieces of 3 cm × 0.6 cm.
5. Spread the dough pieces on a warm surface, dry them 2 or 3 days until they are dryish, turning them over as many times as necessary. Put them into hot oil of about 100℃ until they become swollen and move them to another fry pan to fry them quickly in oil at 150℃.
6. Prepare various dredgings. Apply honey or *choch'ŏng* to the fried *kangjŏng*, and then the prepared dredgings.

7. Chestnut Cookie and jujube Cookie (*Yulran* and *Choran*)

Because of their oval shape, the word, *ran*, is used in the *yulran* and *choran*, which are made from nuts in the shape of an egg.

Ran(卵) cookies are comparable to *cho*(炒) cookies, both of which are made from fruits or their tree roots, which are cooked in honeyed water by boiling down. Then the jam-like substance is mashed and mixed with sugar or honey and moulded into the form of their original fruit. There are three kinds of *ran*, such as the *yulran* with dried chestnut; the *choran* with jujubes and cinnamon; and the *saengkangran* with ginger. The *yulran* is usually made with dried chestnuts in yellows, but these days, fresh chestnuts are also used, adding cinnamon powder. The *choran* is often decorated with pinenuts by studding them onto it.

Fresh, shiny and large jujubes are good and suitable to make the *ran* cookies. When honey is applied to the cookies, it is better to dip them into the honey on a shallow plate with chopsticks and put the crushed pinenut particles onto them. The three different *ran* of chestnuts, jujubes and ginger are very harmonious in color when set on the table and go very well with tea in taste.

On the other hand, *cho* is made with fruits, which are boiled in the honeyed water as they are. Two kinds of *cho* are commonly made, *pamcho* with chestnuts, and *taechucho* with jujubes.

Materials and quantity

chestnut	30 ea
cinnamon power	2 Tbsp
honey	4 Tbsp
minced pinenut	3 Tbsp
jujube	20 ea
cinnamon powder	½ Tbsp
honey	2 Tbsp
pinenut	20 ea

Recipe

Yulran

1. Peel off the hard crust and also the inner crust of the fresh chestnuts, boil them in water, sift, and add cinnamon powder and honey, mix them well and make a lump.
2. Detach a small quantity from the lump, and make a chestnut shaped piece, and put minced pinenut dredg- ing over it.
3. When dried chestnuts are used, grind them to make chestnut powder in advance, then add cinnamon powder and honey to it. The next steps are the same.

Choran

1. Steam the jujubes in the steamer, remove their seed, and knead their meat thoroughly.
2. Add the cinnamon powder and honey to the kneaded jujubes, and put the pan with the mix over low heat. Stir it with a flat wooden scoop while it is being braised. Then make it into a lump of dough.
3. Take a piece from the dough, and make it in the shape of a jujube, and put pinenuts to both ends.

Suggestions

- Fresh jujubes are not suitable for this purpose. Use dried plump jujubes with a lot of meat, which will make the cake mildly palatable.
- In order to apply honey to *yulran*, put honey in a saucer, and cover each piece of *yulran* with honey using chopsticks and then put on minced pinenuts.

8. Ginger Cookie (*Saengran*)

The ginger cookie is called by several different names: the *saengran*, the *kangsaengran*, the *kangran*, etc. This cookie belongs to the category of fruit sweets among the Korean traditional processed fruits or fruit-like sweets.

The ginger cookie is made from ginger starch and ginger juice, with honey. First, fresh ginger is crushed and sifted with a sieve. The juice is let to settle down so that a layer of sediment is formed as starch in the bottom. The juiceless ginger is then mixed with honey and boiled down. When the moisture of the root is gone, ginger starch and honey are poured over it to let it congeal so that all are stuck together. When cooled enough, ginger-like pieces are moulded and dredged with crushed pinenut particles. This ginger cookie, the *saengran*, known as the *kangran*, was enjoyed in the palace, along with the chestnut *yulran* and the jujube *choran*. Among ordinary folks, these cookies were appreciated in various festivities, such as weddings, sixtieth birthdays, wedding anniversary celebrations, and the like.

Ginger has its own particular taste and flavor, so it is used as a seasoning that neutralizes the fishy smell and taste. It strengthens the function of the stomach, and helps soothe vomiting; it also stops coughs and hiccups. When nauseous, candied ginger is good to get rid of such a feeling. Ginger is known to have the effect of stimulating appetites, and help the absorption of nutrients into the body.

Materials and quantity

ginger	400 g
water	1 ½ cups
sugar	½ cup
choch'ŏng or glucose syrup	1 cup
honey	3 Tbsp
pinenut	⅔ cup

Recipe

1. Soak ginger in water and trim it well. Peel off its crust, slice it thin and grind the sliced pieces in a mixer, and sift. Put the sifted ginger syrup into a vessel, and let its sediment form.
2. Put the ginger residue into a kettle, add to it sugar and water of about 2/3 cup, and boil the mix. Remove any foam generated on the surface of the boiling ginger mix, and braise. When the quantity is decreased to half of the original, then add *choch'ŏng* to it, braising it further.
3. When most of the moisture is gone, add honey and ginger sediment to it, and mix them well to the extent it becomes sticky, and then chill it completely.
4. Detach a piece from the lump and make a ginger shaped cookie, and scatter minced pinenuts over it before serving.

Suggestions

- When braising ginger slowly over low heat, make sure it does not get burned.
- Ginger syrup above its sediment can be used for other cakes.
- When mincing the jujube, spread Korean paper and knead it with a knife blade over the paper.

9. Various Color Fruit Cookies (*Kaksaek Chŏngkwa*)

This fruit cake, *chŏngkwa*(正果), is also called *chŏnkwa*(煎果), which is made from soft and juiceless roots, twigs, and fruits. They are boiled down in sugar syrup or caramel until they become chewy and sweet. Fruit cookies are not made one at a time, but several varieties are made at the same time and set up on the table for an assortment of colors.

The commonly used materials for *chŏngkwa* are lotus roots, ginger roots, broad bellflower roots, citron, and figs. Those materials which are not easily come by these days, are winter melon, gourd, hawthorn, and green plum.

This fruit cake, *chŏngkwa*, has various names depending on its major ingredient, such as, *insam chŏngkwa* with ginseng; *yuja chŏngkwa* with citron; *haengin chŏngkwa* with ginkgo seed; *tonga chŏngkwa* with winter melon; *kyul chŏngkwa* with tangerine; *salku chŏngkwa* with plum; *poksunga chŏngkwa* with peach; *aengtu chŏngkwa* with cherry; *mogwa chŏngkwa* with fig; *yŏnkŭn chŏngkwa* with lotus root; *saengkang chŏngkwa* with ginger; *chuksun chŏngkwa* with bamboo shoot; *kŏnp'oto chŏngkwa* with raisin; *murŭt chŏngkwa* with squill root, etc. Besides these, carrot and radish cookies are also made and enjoyed.

These cookies, in various colors, have their own particular taste and flavor, and are also chewy in their own way. These are prepared for the new year's day celebration and for the worship of forefathers. They are enjoyed widely even these days, and can be preserved longer in sugar or invert sugar.

Materials and quantity

fresh broad bellflower root	200 g
sugar	100 g
salt	½ tsp
honey or starchy syrup	4 Tbsp
water	1 ½ cups
ginger	200 g
sugar	100 g
salt	½ tsp
honey	4 Tbsp
water	1 ½ cups
lotus root	200 g
vinegar	½ tsp
sugar	100 g
salt	1 tsp
honey	4 Tbsp
water	1 ½ cups
carrot	200 g
sugar	100 g
salt	½ tsp
honey	4 Tbsp
water	1 ½ cups

Recipe

1. Cut the bellflower root into 4 cm long pieces. Cut thick bellflower root lengthwise first, and then 4 cm long. Dip them in boiling salt water. Peel off the crust of the lotus root, slice it 0. 5 cm thick. Dip in boiling water containing salt and vinegar, and soak and wash lotus pieces in fresh water.
2. Slice the ginger 0. 5 cm thick, and dip the ginger slices in boiling salt water. Also slice the carrot to about 0. 5 cm thick, and then cut the sliced segments further to get 2 cm×4 cm pieces, and dip them in the boiling brine water.
3. Put honey and water to the dipped bellflower root, the lotus root and the carrot, scooping off the foam emerging on the surface. When water content decreases to 1/3, add honey and braise further to give these roots luster. Put the individual roots separately on a rough grid, and chill them.
4. Radish, sliced gourd, or citron can be substituted for the above materials.

10. Cherry Jelly (*Aengtu P'yŏn*)

*K**wapyŏn* means fruit sweets madeŏ from fruits which have a sour taste. The fresh fruit is boiled to be dissolved in water, filtered, boiled down again in honeyed water or sugar solution, congealed to crystalize, and cut into square pieces. A certain fruit juice is slow in congealing; so starch powder is added to hasten the process. This jelly also has several names depending upon its major ingredients, such as, the *aengtu p'yŏn* with cherry; the *pokpunja p'yŏn* with *pokpunja* berry(覆盆子, Rubus coreanus); *salku p'yŏn* with plum; the *omija p'yŏn* with five-flavor seed, *Schizandra chinensis*; etc.

The cherry jelly is made from red ripe cherries, which are boiled in water and filtered. Sugar and green pea starch are added to the juice, boiled again slowly, augmented with honey or jelly, and boiled down again until it becomes a more condensed jelly. In the case of *omija p'yŏn*, the seed must be well soaked in fresh water, and the final product is put into a bowl for cooling.

The most frequently appearing fruit jelly in recorded documents is the cherry jelly, which is often used as a decorating element on ricecakes, or fresh nuts. The cherry is good to make jelly or jam because it is rich in organic acids and pectin contents which help liquid congeal faster, and as such, it has been widely used in making fruit jelly.

Materials and quantity

cherry	5 cups
water	6 cups
green pea starch	1 cup
water	1 cup
salt	¼ tsp
sugar	2 cups

Recipe

1. Wash the cherries, which are in season at the beginning of the summer, add water to them and boil, and sift through a fine grid sieve to obtain cherry juice.
2. Dissolve green pea starch in water, and sift the solution through a fine grid sieve. Add sugar and salt to the cherry juice, and braise. Add the green pea starch solution to the braised cherry juice, and boil over weak heat, stirring continuously. Remove foam emerging on the surface.
3. Braise it to the extent that it becomes jelly, and lower the heat and let it mature. Pour it into a square vessel, let it chill, and put it into the refrigerator for further crystallization.
4. When the cherry jelly is congealed, then cut it, and put it on a plate for serving.

Suggestions

- Any scum or foam while braising, should be scooped off to make a fine looking cherry jelly, *aengtu pyŏn.*
- Cherry jelly gets stickiness and luster when matured or settled after boiling.
- Sour fruits such as strawberry, apricot, and fig may be used for jelly making.
- The cherry attracts insects when wet by the rain. Put the cherries in fresh water, and any insects will come out.

3. Beverages (*Ŭmch'ŏng Lyu,* 飮淸類)

Traditional foods vary a great deal in their kinds, forms, and recipes. According as the ways of living related to food became more and more elaborate and systematized, food came to be developed and classified clearly among three different branches, such as main food, auxiliary food or side dishes, and dessert. The desserts have been diversified, as delicacies, into many varieties and kinds.

The earlier writings on food illustrated numerous food materials, which are used in preparing daily food, delicacies, special food, ceremonial food, and so forth, weaving into the Korean ways of living. The *Karak Kukki*(The Annals of the Karak Kingdom) shows that King Suro offered beverages to the queen's entourage and servants who had escorted the queen safely to get to the king. Here, two sorts of drinks are cited: *lanaek*(蘭液) and *haesŏ*(惠醑). It is not clear what they were, but it is assumed that the former is a kind of soft drink beverage permeated with the flavor of orchids and the latter, a fermented liquor blended with the flavor of orchids.

From this it can be said that Koreans did process herbs and nuts available in their surrounding nature, to make beverages from the earlier times. In a Chinese book on herbs, the *Ponhakcho*(本學草), it already praised Korean five-taste *omija* seed to be the most excellent in quality, and in another Chinese book on herbs, the *Poncho Tokyŏng*(本草圖經), it says, "People dry peppermint from Shilla and enjoy drinking its juice." From these documents, it is easy to conjecture that the five-flavor seed and peppermint were used in beverages in the Three Kingdoms Period in Korea.

According to the *Samkuk Saki*(History of the Three Kingdoms), tea was first introduced from the Tang Dynasty of China to the Korean peninsula during the reign of the 28th ruler, Queen Sŏntŏk of Shilla, i. e., A. D. 632～647: tea seeds were brought in and planted around the Mt. Chilli region. It followed the introduction of Buddhism and its culture, and was spread to, and cherished by, royal families, Buddhist priests, and the young elites, the *wharang*, of the Shilla Kingdom.

Tea drinking mores, which flourished to a large extent, were inherited by the Koryŏ Kingdom which designated Buddhism as the nation saving religion, and as such, tea was served without fail at national ceremonies, such as, *yŏntŭngwhe* with lanterns, *palkwanwhe* for soothing indigenous deity, and *kongtŏkje* to hallow the Buddha.

When Koryŏ was succeeded by Chosŏn, Buddhism was shunned by the new rulers, so the custom of tea drinking also died away with the fall of the Buddhist religion, which was unimaginable during the preceding kingdoms.

On the other hand, the fact that good quality water was available throughout the country, and roasted rice drinks were easily available, must have accelerated the demise of the tea drinking custom outside the temples. It is assumed that at the same time people enjoyed tobacco and liquor as items of fancy. As the saying goes, "Even diluted liquor is better than tea," the liquor drinking custom seems to have been preferred to the tea drinking mores, and became quite common.

There are poems about the hot floor system in the *Tongkuk Isangkuk Chip*(A Collection of Writings of LEE Sang-Kook in Korea, 東國李相國集) and the *Mokŭnchip* (A Collection of Mokŭn's Writing, 牧隱集). From these poems, it is assumed that keeping the rice cooking kettle fixed in the fireplace in the kitchen, along with the very harmonious and ideal setting up of the cooking place and the hot floor for the dual purposes of cooking and floor heating, must have provided a convenient and easy means of making the roast rice drink, *sungnyung*.

The Chosŏn Dynasty period, which witnessed the initiation of elaboration and refinement of Korean traditional food and cuisine, went through the stages of development in techniques of cooking and processing of cakes, cookies, and soft drink beverages, not to mention those in the cookery of main dishes and side dishes as well.

In the cookery book of 1800, *Siŭi Chŏnsŏ*, there are listed numerous beverages, such as, the water boiled cake *sutan*; the sorghum *sutan*; the fermented rice punch *sikhae* and *kamju*; the cinnamon-ginger punch *suchŏngkwa*; the honeyed pear punch *paesuk*; the rose punch *changmi whach'ae*; the azalea punch *tukyŏn whach'ae*; the pear punch *pae whach'ae*; the cherry punch *aengtu whach'ae*; the *pokpunja* berry punch *pokpunja whach'ae*; the peach punch *poksunga whacha'ae*; the water-shield punch *sunch'ae whach'ae*; etc. The book also describes the recipe of the honeyed water punch *milsu*; and of various noodles such as egg noodle *nanmyŏn*, and the *simyŏn* and the corn starch noodle *ch'angmyŏn*. These beverages were developed and widely enjoyed among the ordinary folks but some of them were not listed even in the Korean herbal medicine book *Tongŭi Pokam*.

The most popular traditional drink was ginger tea, followed by the next most cherished ginseng, citron, and fig teas.

1. Fermented Rice Punch (*Sikhae*)

Sikhae is one of the most popular and well known favorites of Koreans. The *Chosŏn Yorihak* boasted, "No quality Chinese tea can be compared with the Korean *sikhae* in the outward look, and esthetic beauty as far as its clear and clean tastes are concerned." Its writer praises, "*Sikhae* helps the digestion, and blood circulation, lessening one's weight, and makes one's mind crystal clear, if one takes it regularly."

The origin of the fermented rice punch may be traced back to the upper layer of *Ye*(禮) of sweet liquid, one of the soft drinks relished by the upper classes of the Chou Dynasty of China, as described in the *Yeki*(禮記). The taste of the rice punch depends on the taste and quality of the barley sprouts which actually ferment juicy rice. In the *Siŭi Chŏnsŏ*(A New Medicinal Series) it describes how to grow barley sprouts. The Korean cookery book, *Chosŏn Yoripŏp*, relates the right size of the barley sprouts: barley sprouts should grow to the size of the length of its grain.

Sikhae is made from regular or glutinous rice, barley sprouts, and honey or sugar. Glutinous rice is digested well, but its grains contract and therefore do not float onto the surface of the punch and taste coarse in the mouth. They also tend to stick to the mouth. There is a variety of *sikhae*, called *sŏkkamju* (夕甘酒), which is made from a mixture of rice, brown sugar, honey and barley sprouts, and boiled until the rice becomes red in color. The *sikhae* of the sifted rice, garnished with pinenuts or sliced jujubes is offered, first of all, as a sacrifice to forefathers, and served as a dessert of a meal.

Materials and quantity

malt or barley sprout	4 cups
rice	5 cups
water	20 cups
sugar	3 cups
ginger(citron syrup)	1 root(50 g)
pinenut	2 Tbsps

Suggestions

- When buying barley sprouts, avoid getting old ones and dark colored ones.
- In order to have all rice particles emerge to the surface of the juice, it is important to wash the boiled rice well and drain off the water completely.

Recipe

1. Soak malt in warm water, rub it with hands, sift it and allow it to settle down. When its sediment is formed, scoop out its clear juice over the sediment.
2. Wash rice, and steam it rather dryish, add malt juice to the steamed rice, and leave the mix for 4~5 hours at a temperature of 65℃.
3. When several rice particles emerge on the surface, parboil it, take out all the rice, put it into cold water to remove its sweet taste. Drain off the water and remove as much remaining moisture as possible.
4. Add sugar to the juice and boil it. Remove any scum while boiling. Add ginger pieces to it and boil it again. Sweetened citron, instead of ginger, may be used; let the flavor of citron permeate sufficiently into the juice; in this case, too, only the juice is used, leaving the citron filtered out.
5. Chill the juice, pour it into a vessel, float the chilled rice, and serve.

2. Cinnamon-Ginger Punch (*Suchŏngkwa,* 水正果)

Besides the common name *suchŏngkwa*, this Korean traditional cinnamon-ginger punch is called *suchŏnkwa*, which is made from boiled down juice of cinnamon and ginger, to which sugar is added, then cooled, and garnished with a dried persimmon, pears or floating pinenuts.

The major ingredients used in the punch, are pomegranate, citron, sweet potato, ginger, dried persimmons, lotus blossom, five-flavor *omija*, *tuchung*(杜冲), hawthorn, cherry, etc. Honey is for sweetening, and pinenuts, for garnishing. The five-flavor seed *omija* and rouge *yŏnji* are used for coloring.

Dried persimmons, which are used quite often in the punch, give the punch a clear taste and flavor; but the soft and sweet persimmon makes it more palatable. The persimmon is not added when the punch is being boiled because it may make the punch opaque and dull; therefore, it is added immediately before the serving by moisturizing it with honeyed water or punch to the extent that it becomes soft, and then it is put into the punch. A quality persimmon has a white powder covering on its crust. Its seeds and peduncle must be removed.

On the other hand, ginger and cinnamon are not boiled together lest they should lose their own flavors; consequently they are boiled separately and mixed together when cooled for a better combination of tastes.

The icy cinnamon-ginger punch tastes better when it is served in a warm room in the winter.

Materials and quantity

dried persimmon	20 ea
walnut	10 ea
ginger	100 g
water	20 cups
cinnamon bark	60 g
brown sugar	1 cup
white sugar	1 cup
pinenut	2 Tbsp

Recipe

1. Wipe off the dried persimmons with a wet cloth, take off the peduncles, and remove the seeds.
2. Crack the hard crust of the walnuts, add their meat to the persimmons, and roll with a seaweed roller screen to make the persimmon roll round.
3. Peel off the crust of the ginger, wash it, shred it, add 10 cups of water to it, boil it over low heat to have its fragrance come off into the water. Wash the cinnamon bark, add 10 cups of water to it, boil it sufficiently, and sift it through a fine net sieve with the ginger juice.
4. Add sugar to the mixed juice. Slice the persimmons into 1 cm thick pieces.
5. Pour the mixed juice into a vessel, and put the persimmons with walnuts into the mixed juice and serve.

Suggestions

- The ginger and hard cinnamon can be boiled together to make *suchŏngkwa*, but it is better to boil them separately and mix them later, which will help make their individual and particular flavors and tastes stand out separately.
- When rolling of the persimmon is not desired, take off its seeds, and cut it into two if the persimmon is large, and pour a little amount of ginger juice into a small vessel and soak it in the juice about 30 minutes before serving.
- Recently harvested dried persimmons dissolve easily, so adjust the soaking time before serving.

3. Azalea Punch (*Chintalrae Whach'ae*)

Azalea punch is made with azalea flower petals gathered from the hills and mountains during the spring, which are then covered with starch and fried. The fried blossoms are then floated onto the five-flavor *omija* juice made from its well ripened seeds. Azalea punch is recorded in the *Kyukon Yoram*, where *chintalrae whach'ae* is introduced as "the representative spring punch."

According to both the *Tongkuk Saesiki* and *Yŏlyang Saesiki*, the forefathers of Koreans went on a picnic to enjoy and appreciate the spring flowers on March the third by the lunar calendar. There, they gathered azalea flowers to make flower fry, by kneading glutinous rice flour with them. They also made the azalea punch with new fresh azalea flowers.

When you soak *omija* in water, do not use hot water lest it should taste sour and astringent; but first, boil water and let cool, into which put *omija*, let it soak slowly and sufficiently over the night. The taste and flavor of *omija* vary according to the quality and kind of its seeds; consequently, it is important to adjust the balance of the ingredients of the punch properly.

After a delicious and gorgeous meal is served, a punch augments the feeling of satisfaction of the main course of the meal, and also helps digest food already consumed.

Materials and quantity

omija(five-flavor) seed	1 cup
water(boiled and chilled)	12 cups
honey	1 cup
sugar syrup	⅔ cup
azalea flower	20 blossoms
green pea starch	2 Tbsp
pinenut	1 Tbsp

❶

❷

❸

❹

Recipe

1. Boil water and chill it, and then put *omija* seeds into the water, soak it overnight. When its juice turns pink to the color of azalea, sift it through a fine grid sieve.
2. Add honey and sugar syrup to the juice, adjusting the color and taste of the mix.
3. Cover the azalea petals with green pea starch, dip them in boiling water and let cool in fresh water. As such, they will be soft and will pass through the throat gently.
4. Pour *omija* juice into a glass vessel up to 70% of the space, and float the azalea flower petals and pinenuts.

Suggestions

- If one does not find the *omija* juice palatable, it is better to dilute the juice by maintaining the proportion of the juice and water at 1:16.
- When soaking out *omija* seeds, be sure to use a vessel with no traces of oil.
- Instead of normal starch powder, use green pea starch, which makes the azalea flower petals softer and more tender.
- No change of color occurs, optimally, when the azalea flower petals covered with green pea starch is dipped into water for only 1 or 2 seconds, and cooled in fresh water.

4. Citron Punch (*Yuja Whach'ae*)

Whach'ae punch is usually served with tea on the tea table and enjoyed as a dessert drink as part of the meal. Citron punch is made from the crust of a citron, its meat, and pomegranate seeds, which are rich in flavor and taste. *Yuja whach'ae* is prepared by putting sliced pears, red pomegranate seeds, and pinenuts into a vessel and pouring honey or sugar over them so that they will float onto the surface. The punch tastes better when served cold. In other words, this citron punch consists of honeyed citron meat, sliced citron crust, pomegranate seeds, and sliced pears floated on the sweetened water-all of which give a feeling permeated with the autumn mood that one may cherish.

The outer crust of the citron is rough, but gives off a pleasant scent. This is the fruit, among the orange type fruits, which can help withstand a cold more than any other Oriental fruit.

Citron *yuja*, according to the *Pangyak Happ'yŏn*, tastes sweet, and augments the taste of liquor, stimulates warmth in the body, eliminates bad air from the stomach, and lightens a hangover. The vitamin C content in the citron is bountiful, and, as such, it has been used from earlier times as a drug to cure a cold. It also accelerates the recuperation from fatigue and hangovers.

It is advisable to preserve the citron punch cold and drink it cold after the meal, which leaves a pleasant taste in the mouth.

Materials and quanity

citron .... 2 ea
pear .... 1 ea
pomegranate seed .... 2 Tbsp
pinenut .... 3 Tbsp
sugar syrup .... 3 cups
(sugar 1 cup+water 3 cups)

Suggestions

- Wash the citron well, because it is going to be processed and eaten raw.
- Cool the punch sufficiently to the extent that one feels its chilliness even with one's teeth.
- Pour the punch into a vessel, taking care that the citron meat will not be disturbed and dispersed.
- Obtain the citrons when they are in season. Wash them, wipe off the moisture, and dry them. Mince them to 0. 2 cm~0. 3 cm thick, add sugar or honey and store away, and use them to make citron tea or thick rice cake, *tut'ŏp ttŏk.*

Recipe

1. Cut each citron into 4 pieces lengthwise, remove its meat and seeds, and cut again each divided crust into 2 or 3 pieces.
2. Separate the outer crust from the inner soft and tender meat with a knife, and mince the outer crust minutely. Peel a pear, and slice it to the size of the minced citron crust.
3. Put sugar into water and boil the mix, cool it, and add honey to it to make punch.
4. Put the minced citron and pear close to the surrounding edge of a vessel, put pomegranate and citron meat, and pinenuts in the center, and pour punch slowly into the vessel. Let fragrance of the citron ooze out for a while and then serve.

5. *Omija* Punch (五味子花菜)

The five-flavor *omija* punch is made from *omija* seeds which are soaked in fresh water to make juice.

The solution becomes pink like the color of azalea flowers. The Korean *omija* is well known for its quality, and widely used in various types of punches.

When dried, good quality *omija* is tinged with a red color, and sticky. As time goes by, the color turns from bright red into dark brown.

Therefore the red *omija* is fresh and good for making savory punch, giving it a dry and light taste because *omija* brings about a good combination of various flavors of sundry ingredients.

Omija is rich in tannin and has an astringent taste. The color changes when boiled, and therefore care must be taken lest it should be dull in taste and appearance. The outer crust of the *omija* seed tastes sweet and sour as well. The core of its seed is hot, salty and bitter. From these five flavors, the *omija* picked up its name.

Its meat is analyzed as an invigorating tonic, and for removing phlegm, neutralizing thirstiness, and stimulating the lung functions. It is especially good for curing a cold and thirstiness.

The representative punches that use the *omija* are the pear, barley ball, rose, water lily, azalea punches, and *chŏngmyŏn*(청면).

Materials and quantity

omija(five-flavor) seed	1 cup
water(boiled and cooled)	½ cup
honey	1 cup
sugar syrup	⅔ cup
pear	1 ea
pinenut	1 Tbsp

Recipe

1. Boil *omija* in water, cool it, soak it in fresh water over night until the pink azalea color is soaked out. Extract its juice by sifting it with a fine double grid sieve.
2. Add honey and sugar syrup to the extracted five-flavor juice, and adjust its taste and color.
3. Peel off the crust of the pear, slice it and trim the sliced pieces in the shape of a pear blossom. Put the trimmed pear pieces into honey or sugar syrup. Trim pinenuts, taking off any inner skin pieces.
4. Pour chilled *omija* juice into a glass or ceramic vessel, and float pear pieces and pinenuts over the *omija* juice. Seasonwise, different fruit pieces can be floated.

Suggestions

- Use only well ripened *omija*. Otherwise, you cannot get rich color and palatable taste of the five-flavor seeds soaked out.
- Prepare a lot of *omija* extraction at a time for better taste and finer color. Concoct sugar syrup with an equal amount of sugar and water.
- No oil nor its trace especially on the vessel should be allowed to get into the *omija* juice when it is being processed.
- Instead of pear pieces in a pear blossom shape to be floated on the juice, its round or sliced pieces can also make beautiful floaters.
- Pour *omija* juice in a bottle, keep it in the refrigerator and serve with fruit floater, conveniently.

6. Pine Pollen Punch (*Songwha Milsu*, 松花蜜水)

Koreans have consumed the pollen of flowers as food. Pine flower pollen has seen various uses of its own; the pattern- pressed pastry of pine pollen, *songwha dasik*, is made from pine pollen and honey, whose dough is pressed onto the pattern; this is relished as one of the delicacies at a wedding or other celebration. The pollen can be made into pine pollen tea dissolved in hot water by putting pine pollen in a silk bag and placing it in hot water.

Pine pollen punch is an ideal drink in the summer, made from pine pollen dissolved in hot water, to which honey is added, and pinenuts used as garnish on it. The reason that this punch is much relished, is that it dispels or lightens the feeling of warmth in the summer, giving off its particular aroma.

There is a saying, "Drink pine pollen punch with pinenuts regularly in the summer, and you will enjoy the longevity of life." Pine pollen is said to stimulate lung functions, divert ill feelings, prevent palsy, and stop bleeding.

At the same time, honey is also effective in overcoming the summer heat. Not only does honey have such an effect, but it also helps lighten one's stress. Dark colored honey is mainly used in drugs, while transparent honey is used in food. The honey commonly used in punch is bush clover, acacia, and rape honeys.

Materials and quantity

pine pollen powder	½ cups
water(boiled and cooled)	4 cups
honey	9 Tbsp
pinenut	1 Tbsp

Recipe

1. Pluck pine blossoms in full bloom in the early part of June, and dry them in a large wooden container. Beat off their pollen over a large earthenware with water. Soak it in fresh water in an earthenware for 3 days, changing the water every day to get rid of its bitter taste. Spread a bamboo mat and place a cloth over it, and spread the pine pollen over it for drying.
2. Boil water, cool it, and add honey to it.
3. Put pine pollen into the honeyed syrup, and stir to dissolve the pollen, and float the pinenuts. From the punch fresh pine fragrance expands out dimly.

Suggestions

- The taste, fragrance, color and density of honey differ according to the season when it is harvested. Dark honey is used in medicine, and white honey is used in punch or for food seasoning.
- During the summer, pine pollen punch with honey helps dispel thirstiness easily. Do not dissolve pine pollen far in advance of serving, for it sinks to the bottom, forming a sediment. Therefore, dissolve it immediately before serving.

7. Round Rice Ball Punch (*Wŏnsopyŏng*, 元宵餅, 圓小餅)

W*ŏnsopyŏng* is a punch made from glutinous rice flour in several colors, kneaded into colored balls, dipped in boiling water, and floated onto honeyed water or *omija* extracted juice.

This punch is mainly prepared for the new year's day celebration. The name of this punch is derived from its initiator named *Wŏnso*(元宵) living in Beijing, who prepared it for the new year's day. From his initiation, the custom of preparing it on the new year's day has become a part of the celebration that the people follow. Its second homophonous name is derived, or interpreted, from its small size and round(圓小) shape.

The round ball punch, which was made at Changdŏk Palace of the Chosŏn Dynasty, belongs to the same category as *ttŏk sutan*(cereal ball punch), but was prepared on January the 15th, instead.

In order to make an oozing and fine punch, the glutinous rice flour should be dyed lightly. When dipped in boiling honeyed liquid, rice balls taste better because they are infiltrated by the sweet element. Kneading should be done using cold water, avoiding using warm water which makes the dough too stretchy. *Wŏnsopyŏng* punch tastes very fragrant when a spoonful of honeyed citron liquid is added.

This traditional punch is fine in its color and its rice ball is chewy, so it tastes delicious during the summer, and also goes well with the rice and soup prepared for the new year's day.

Materials and quantity

glutinous rice	1 ½ cups(powder, 3cups)
salt	¼ tsp
gardenia seed	2 ea
omija seed	⅓ cup
mugwort powder	1 Tbsp
stuffing	
jujube	15 ea
tangerines syrup	2 Tbsp
citron syrup	2 Tbsp
starch powder	½ cup
punch	
honey or sugar	1 cup
water	4 cups
pinenut	1 Tbsp

Suggestions

- When gardenia seeds, five-flavor seeds, and mugwort are not available, color additives may be used as substitutes.
- Do not pour too much water into the rice powder when kneading; excessive moisture tends to make the dough ball deformed, which will not stay round.

Recipe

1. Add salt to the glutinous rice powder, sift it, and divide it into 4 portions.
2. Add gardenia seed juice to one portion, *omija*(five-fragrance) seed juice to another portion, and the mugwort powder to a third portion and leave a fourth portion as it is so that you will get four different color powers: yellow, red, green and white. Pour boiling water to each, and knead it to make the four different colored dough.
3. Remove the seed and crust from the jujubes. The tangerines in syrup and the citron in syrup are then put together and minced to make stuffing.
4. Put the stuffing into the kneaded dough, and make it into a round ball of 2 cm in diameter.
5. Cover the dough balls with the starch powder, and boil them in water, then put them into fresh water, scoop out, and remove the moisture.
6. Put these colored balls into a punch vessel, add chilled honey or sugar syrup, and spray pinenuts to float on the surface.

❷

❸

❹

❺

Glossary

aengtu pyŏng: cherry jelly
changmi whajŏn: fried rose flower cake
chapkwapyŏng: multi-fruit cake
chijinŭn ttŏk: pan-fried cake
chintalrae whach'ae: azalea punch
chintalrae whajŏn: pan-fried azalea flower cake
ch'inŭn ttŏk: pounded cake
choran: jujube cookie
chuak: deep fried cake
chŭngp'yŏn: fermented rice-cake
hopak ttŏk: cucumber cake
injŏlmi: sticky rice-cake
kaep'i ttŏk: wind cake
kaksaek chŏngkwa: multi-colored fruit cookies
kaksaek kyŏngdan: multi-colored rice ball
kaksaekp'yŏn: colored cake
kangjŏng: taffy pop cookie
kolmu ttŏk: thimble cake
k'ong siruttŏk: steamed bean cake
kkot chŏlp'yŏn: flower cake
kukwha jŏn: pan-fried chrysanthemum flower cake
kyŏndan(=*tanja*): rice ball
maejakkwa: plum sparrow cookie
maenturami whajŏn: pan-fried cockscomb flower cake
mujige ttŏk: rainbow cake, multi-colored cake
mu siruttŏk: steamed radish cake
noktu p'yŏn: green pea cake
omegi ttŏk: glutinous millet cake
omija: five-flavored seed
paek sŏlki: white powder rice-cake
pamch'o: honeyed chestnut
pam tanja: chestnut rice ball(cake)
p'atkomul siruttŏk: steamed redbean rice-cake
sanja: taffy pop cookie
saengran: ginger cookie
saek tanja: multi-color rice ball cake
saek ttŏk: multi-colored cake; rainbow cake

sikhae: fermented rice punch
sŏki tanja: stone mushroom rice ball(cake)
songpyŏn: pine cake; half-moon shaped stuffed cake
songwha milsu: pine pollen punch
sŏpsan sampyŏng: fried *tŏtŏk* cake
ssuk tanja: wormwood rice ball cake
suchŏngkwa: cinnamon-ginger punch
susu pukkumi: sorghum stuffed cake
sutan: rice ball punch
taech'uch'o: honeyed jujube
taech'u tanja: jujube rice ball cake
tanja: rice ball(cake)
tasik: pattern-pressed pastry
tchinttŏk: steamed rice-cake
ttŏk: rice(cereal)-cake
tut'ŏp tanja: thick ball cake
tut'ŏp ttŏk: thick cake
ŭnhaeng tanja: gingko rice ball(cake)
whach'ae: punch
whajŏn: pancake with flower petal decorations
wŏnsopyŏng: round rice ball punch
yakkwa: fried cookie
yaksik: honeyed rice-cake
yŏtkanngjŏng: taffy cookie
yuja whach'ae: citron punch
yulran: chestnut cookie

INDEX

E

F

G

H

I

J

K

References

1. HŎ Kyun, *Tomun Taejak*(屠門大嚼), 1611.
2. CHANG Ji-Young (of Antong), *Kyukon Siŭipang*(閨壼是議方), Revised and edited by WHANG Hye-Sŏng, Hankook Insŏ Publisher, 1981.
3. CHANG of Antong, *Ŭmsik Chimibang*(飮食知味方), 1670.
4. Author Unknown, *Yorok*(要錄), 1680.
5. Scholar HA, *Chubangmun*(酒方文), Toward the end of 1600s.
6. HONG Man-Sŏn, *Sanrim Kyŏngje*(山林經濟, Economics of Mountain-Forrest), 1715.
7. RYU Tŭk-Kong, *Kyŏngto Chapji*(京都雜志), 1747～1800.
8. RYU Chung-Im, *Chŭngpo Sanrim Kyŏngje*(증보산림경제, Revised Mountain-Forest Economy), 1766.
9. KIM Mae-Sun, *Lyŏlyang Sesiki*(洌陽歲時記), 1777.
10. SŎ Yu-Ku *Onghŭi Chapji*(甕饎雜志), 1800s.
11. LEE of Pinghŏkak(憑虛閣), *Kyuhap Ch'ongsŏ*(閨閤叢書), 1815, Translated and annotated by CHUNG Lyang-Wan, Pojinje, 1986.
12. SŎ Yu-Ku, *Imwon Sipyukji*(林園十六誌), 1827.
13. HONG Sŏk-Mo, *Tongkuk Sesiki*(東國歲時記), Translated and annotated by CH'OE Tae-Lim, Hongsin Munwha-sa, 1934.
14. Author Unknown, *Yŏkjupangmun*(歷酒方文), Middle of 1800s.
15. Author Unknown, *Umshikpŏp*(飮食法), 1854.
16. Author Unknown, *Siŭijŏnsŏ*(是議全書), Middle of 1800s.
17. Author Unknown, *Puin Pilji*(夫人必知), 1855.
18. PANG Sin-Yŏng, *Chosŏn Yoripŏp*(朝鮮料理法), Hansŏng Tosŏ Chusikhoesa, 1913.
19. CHO Cha-Ho, *Chosŏn Yoripŏp*, Kwanghan-Sŏrim, 1938.
20. SON Chŏng-Kyu, *Chosŏn Yori*(Korean Cooking), Ilhan-Sŏpang, 1940.
21. LEE Yong-Ki, *Chosŏn Mussang Sinsik Yorijepŏp* (Unique and New Korean Cookery), Yŏngchang-Sŏkwan, 1943.
22. Author Unknown, *Siŭibang*(是議方), 1945.
23. BANG Sin-Yŏng, *Urinara Yoriŭi Mantŭnŭn Pŏp* (Korean Cookery), 1952.
24. BANG Sin-Yŏng, *Yoriŭi Mantŭnŭn Pŏp* (Cookery), Changch'ung Tosŏ Ch'ulph'an-sa.
25. HAN Hŭi-Sun et al, *Yicho Kungchung Yori T'ongko*(A Survey of Food of Royal Court of the Yi-Danasty), Hakch'ong-sa. 1957.
26. *Hyŏndae Yŏsŏng Paekwa Sajŏn*(Modern Encyclopedia for Woman), 1969.
27. WHANG Hye-Sŏng, *Kungchung Yori*(Food of Royal Court), 1972.
28. CHŎNG Yak-Yŏng, *Aŏnkakbi*(雅言覺非), Translated and annotated by KIM Chong-Kwŏn, Ilji-sa, 1972.
29. *Hankuk Minsok Chonghap Chosa Pokosŏ*(A Comprehensive Report on Korean Folklore), Cultural Assets Management Bureau, Ministry of Cultural Affairs, 1977.
30. KANG In-Hŭi, *Hankukŭi Siksaengwhalsa*(A History of the Korean Dietary Life), Samyŏng-sa, 1978.
31. LEE Sŏng-Wu, *Hankukŭi Sikkyŏng Taejŏn*(韓國食經大全), Hyangmun-sa, 1981.
32. KIM Hak-Wun, *Hankukŭi Ch'aŭi Munwha* (Korean Tea Culture), Hyŏnam-sa, 1981.
33. LEE Sŏng-Wu, *Hankukŭi Sikp'umŭi Munwhasa* (A Cultural History of Korean Food), Kyomun-sa. 1984.
34. LEE Sŏng-Wu, *Hankukŭi Yori Munwha*(Korean Cuisine Culture), Kyomun-sa, 1985.
35. Yun Sŏsŏk, *Hankukŭi Sikp'umsa Yŏnku*(A Historical Study of Korean Food Stuff), Sinkwang Publisher, 1985.
36. WANG Chun-Ryŏn, *Hankukŭi Yori Paekkwa* (III) (The Encyclopedia of Korean Food (III), Pŏmhan Publisher, 1986.
37. YUN Sŏ-Sŏk, *Hankukŭi Yori*(Korea Cuisine), Suhak-sa, 1986.
38. WHANG Hye-Sŏng, *Chŏnt'ongŭi Mat, Ttŏk, Hankwaja, Umryo*(Traditional Taste, Rice-cake, Korean Cookies, and Beverages), Chupusaengwhal-sa, 1986.
39. KANG In-Hŭi, *Hankukŭi Mat*(Korean Flavor), Taehan Kyokwasŏ Chusikhoe-sa, 1987.

40. YŎM Ch'o-Ae, CHANG Myŏng-Suk & YOON Suk-Ja, *Hankuk Yori*(Korean Cuisine), Hyoil Munwha-sa, 1992.
41. YOON Suk-Ja, *Hankukŭi Chŏnt'ong Yori: Uritŭlŭi Mat*(Korean Traditional Cuisine: Korean Flavor), Kangwon Ilbo-sa, 1990.
42. YU Tae-Jong, *Sikp'um Pokam*(Handbook of Food), Munwun-sa, 1988.
43. *Hankukŭi Ttŏk Munwhaŭi Yŏnku*(Studies on Korean Rice-cake Culture), Kim Kyŏng-Jin Kyosu Chŏngnyŏn Kinyŏm Chunpi Ŭiwonhŭi, 1998.
44. CHANG Ki-Suk, Yakkwaŭi Choriŭi T'ŭksŏnge Kwanhan Yŏngku(A Study on the Characteristics of the *Yakkwa* Cooking), MA Thesis, Sŏngsin Women's University, 1977.
45. LEE Chŏl-Ho & MAENG Yŏng-Sŏn, "Hankukŭi Kwajalyuŭi Munhŏnjŏk Koch'al(A Bibliographical Study of Korean Sweets." *Hankuk Sikmunwha Hakhŭiji* 2. 1, 1987.
46. LEE Ch'ŏl-Ho & MAENG Yŏng-Sŏn, "Hankukŭi Ttŏke Kwanhan Munhŏnjŏk Koch'al(A Bibliographical Study on Korea Rice-cake)", *Hankuk Sikmunwhaji*, 2.2. 1987.
47. CHO Sin-Ho & LEE Hyŏ-Ji, "Hankwaja Munwhaŭi Pyŏnch'ŏne Kwanhan Munhŏnjŏk Koch'al(A Bibliographical Study on the Vicissitudes of Korean Sweets Culture)," *Hankuk Sikmunwha Hakhŭiji*, 2. 1, 1987.
48. YUN Tŏk-In, Hankukkwa Ilponŭi Ttŏklyuŭi Pyŏnch'ŏn-Paltale Kwanhan Pikyo Yŏnku, (A Comparative Study on the Development and Changes betweenn the Korean and Japanese Rice-cakes, Chungang University Ph.D. disseration, 1987.
49. MAENG Hye-Lyŏl, LEE Hyo-Ji, "Ttŏklyuŭi Munwhajŏk Koch'al, (A Bibliographical Survey of Rice-cakes", *Hankuk Sikmunwha Hakhoeji*, 3.3, 1988.
50. LEE Ch'ŏl-Ho et al., "Hankukŭi Chŏnt'ong Ŭmlyoe Kwanhan Munhŏnjŏk Koch'al (A Bibliographical Study of Korean Traditional Beverages)", *Hankuk Sikmunwha Hankhoeji*, 6.1, 1991.